COMMISSION OF THE EUROPEAN COMMUNITIES

1992 and beyond

by John Palmer

DOCUMENT

9100025403

NOTICE

This publication, designed to contribute to public debate on European integration, was prepared outside the Commission of the European Communities. The views expressed are those of the author alone, and do not necessarily reflect the opinion of the Commission.

This publication is also available in:

ES   ISBN 92-826-0126-9
DA   ISBN 92-826-0127-7
DE   ISBN 92-826-0128-5
GR   ISBN 92-826-0129-3
FR   ISBN 92-826-0130-7
IT   ISBN 92-826-0131-5
NL   ISBN 92-826-0132-3
PT   ISBN 92-826-0133-1

Cataloguing data appear at the end of this publication

Luxembourg: Office for Official Publications of the European Communities, 1989

ISBN 92-826-0088-2

Catalogue number: CB-56-89-861-EN-C

Contents

Preface and acknowledgements   5

Chapter 1 — Setting the scene   7

Chapter 2 — The cost of 'non-Europe' 21

Chapter 3 — Relaunching Europe 37

Chapter 4 — The new agenda 47

Chapter 5 — Will it all happen? 61

Chapter 6 — Towards Europe 2000 77

Preface and acknowledgements

This is a book which started off as an account of '1992', the date which has become the nearly universal symbol of the completed European internal market. In the months which followed the invitation from the European Commission to write the book, a much wider and more long-term debate about the future of the European Community has taken off. Inevitably, I have been infected with the excitement which this debate has engendered and thus it has become less a historical account of the genesis of the single market and rather more an attempt to examine the different futures which may be on offer for the peoples of Europe up to and beyond 1992.

My thanks are due to the Commission not only for having asked me to write the book but for having insisted that it should be a purely personal view of the future. I am grateful for having been given complete freedom to express personal opinions and judgments — not all of which the Commission will endorse. I must also express my warm thanks to my former colleague, Alex Scott, for all his help in turning this project into reality and to a variety of friends working in the European Community institutions who, alas, must remain anonymous, but who gallantly undertook to read the manuscript and correct my grosser errors. It goes without saying that they are in no way responsible for any residual errors of fact or judgment nor for the sometimes controversial views I pronounce on aspects of Community affairs. Sincere thanks are also due to Gay Kavanagh for all her efforts, without which no intelligible manuscript would ever have emerged at all. Finally a word of appreciation to my long-suffering family and friends for putting up with the stresses and strains of this book's gestation.

Chapter 1

Setting the scene

'May you live in interesting times', says the old Chinese greeting. Well these are not just interesting but exciting times to be reporting and analysing European affairs.

After years of stagnation and introspection, Europe is experiencing major economic and political changes. There is an evident mood among peoples in most Community countries for greater European unity. Recent steps, however hesitant, towards closer European integration are being taken far more seriously by the outside world than at any time since the early 1950s.

I speak of 'Europe'. But of course this begs the question: what Europe? There are still several different 'Europes' and it is as well to be clear from the start about whom we are talking. This book deals with developments in the 12-nation European Community and specifically the project to complete a single European market of more than 300 million people by the end of 1992.

The European Community forms the economic and political core of western Europe and is, increasingly, also an economic and political magnet for many of the countries of central and eastern Europe. So the story of the 1992 market — and the much wider economic, political and social changes which are being generated in its wake — is one that intimately affects Europe as a whole.

This is one reason why, for example, the six nations of the European Free Trade Association are so keen to negotiate a 'common European economic space' with the countries of the EC. And it also helps to explain both the agreement on mutual recognition by the European Community and the Council for Economic Cooperation (Comecon) and the negotiations of new trade and cooperation agreements between the EC and individual Comecon States. Such agreements have now been signed between the Community and both Hungary and Poland.

The single European market project is, of course, primarily, to do with the commercial, economic and industrial life of the Community. But its evolution and the parallel policies designed to encourage EC integration are, as we shall see, likely to transform the economies of not only the EC countries but, to a greater or lesser extent, those of other western and possibly even eastern European countries who seek a closer association with the Community in the 1990s.

The decision to implement the single European market was not taken in a political vacuum.

The 12 Member States of the Community have also agreed, in some cases not without considerable domestic political difficulty, to amend the Treaty of Rome — the founding constitution of the EC — in ways that have put the longer term goals of European unity firmly back on the political agenda.

One of the most important provisions of the Single European Act (SEA) is to increase the range of political decisions taken by the EC Council of Ministers on the basis of a majority vote. The Council of Ministers is the body in Community affairs which passes the laws on the basis of policy proposals from the Commission and after consultation with the directly elected European Parliament which binds the 320 million people of the 12 EC countries.

These and other changes ushered in by the SEA — including an enhanced role in influencing legislation for the European Parliament — and the planned implementation of the European 'social dimension' have sparked a major political debate throughout the Member States on the longer term future of the Community. In the process many new questions are being raised about the direction which should be taken by the Community.

Is the single market merely a matter of eliminating direct and indirect barriers to free trade and the free movement of capital, people and services? Will the market have to be accompanied by the extension of minimum social provision for the working people and will there have to be greater provision for the rights of European citizens to live and work wherever they wish in the Community?

Can you really have a single internal market subject to the same rules on competition and with complete freedom of movement of capital without a much more developed European Monetary System? Indeed can the Community for much longer delay having a monetary system in which all national currencies are equally involved, in which a single European currency is progressively introduced and in which monetary policy is coordinated by a supranational body such as a European central bank?

Will the single market and these related developments leave essentially untouched the present balance of political sovereignty between national States and the European Community? Conversely will these developments, to say nothing of the evolution of cooperation in policy areas such as foreign affairs and security, not propel the Community quite rapidly down the road to economic and eventually, to political union?

Some European Community leaders already believe something like this may have already become inevitable. The President of the Commission, Mr Jacques Delors, told Members of the European Parliament in June 1988, that the Community might have to develop 'the embryo of a European government' during the 1990s and he predicted that, in any event, the Community would be responsible for some '80% of economic and social legislation'.

It was predictions of this kind, together with the reaffirmation by other EC leaders of their commitment to eventual federal union, which stimulated the intervention in the debate of the UK Prime Minister, Mrs Margaret Thatcher. Speaking in Bruges during September 1988,

Mrs Thatcher made clear her opposition to anything smacking of a federal union, which she described as a threat not only to national political sovereignty but even to the separate national and cultural identity of the different peoples of the EC.

This view has been strongly contested by most other EC Heads of State or Government as well as by long-standing supporters of European union. When they met in Brussels during October 1988, the leaders of the Christian Democrat-led governments of Belgium, the Federal German Republic, the Netherlands, Italy and Luxembourg reiterated their backing for the kind of supranational Community envisaged in the Treaty of Rome — and reiterated in the SEA — and even suggested the need to evolve a European Security Union.

The debate on the future of Europe is now well and truly under way. Thus far it has mainly been the preserve of politicians and professional policy advisers and decision-makers. But it is also gradually being taken up by political parties across the ideological spectrum in the Community — both in the European Parliament and in the different national legislatures.

It is obvious that the new perspectives for the European Community have been stimulated primarily by internal economic and political factors. But it would be wrong to ignore the profound impact on thinking about the future of the European Community which events in the outside world are having.

Recent years have seen dramatic changes, for example in the European security environment. Under President Reagan, the United States has taken a number of steps, including encouragement for the Strategic Defence Initiative, which some Europeans see as a symbol of a new American aspiration for greater self-reliance for its own defence and a potential cause of a future destabilization in the balance of military power between the super-powers.

At the same time, the grave financial crisis which has affected the US Federal Government budget and the foreign trade balance has encouraged the conviction that a future American administration may be obliged to make major savings in expenditure on the defence of western Europe. There have been persistent suggestions that the US, under certain circumstances, might be ready to run down the present scale of its commitment in terms of US forces stationed in western Europe, with or without an agreement with the Warsaw Pact reducing the overall level of conventional forces deployed by NATO and the Warsaw Pact in Europe. The likelihood of this appeared to increase after the announcement of unilateral reductions in forces made by the Soviet President, Mr Mikhail Gorbachev in December 1988.

The Reykjavik Summit meeting between President Reagan and Mr Gorbachev, in November 1986, also excited fears among some of America's NATO allies in Europe, that Washington was becoming less sensitive to European views about Alliance defence and arms control strategy. These developments directly encouraged both the revival of the Western European Union, a forum of seven of the 12 EC Member States who are also members of NATO, with the objective of encouraging a 'stronger European pillar in the Atlantic Alliance'. Indeed, the WEU seven became 'nine' in 1988 with the accession of Portugal and Spain.

At the same time there have been far-reaching changes on the other side of the Iron Curtain. The emergence of Mr Gorbachev has led to the most radical attempts at economic restructuring and political reform seen in the Soviet Union for more than half a century.

The impact of *perestroika* and *glasnost* has been paralleled by a striking improvement in relations between the super-powers. This was reflected in the agreement by the United States and the Soviet Union in 1987, to withdraw all their land-based intermediate-range nuclear forces from Europe and also in the separate attempts to negotiate major reductions in strategic nuclear, chemical and conventional forces.

These developments have intimately affected the debate within Europe. For example, in the post-INF age and in the context of possible new arms-control agreements, should Western Europe reconsider traditional notions of its defence and its appreciation of a 'Soviet threat'? Indeed does any such threat exist at all?

How far should the European Community go in identifying itself with and assisting the process of economic reform in both the Soviet Union and the countries of Eastern Europe? Are major new possibilities emerging for joint ventures in these countries between European private and Soviet State-owned enterprises?

These questions are pregnant with political implications. Some see in them a temptation by EC countries such as the Federal Republic of Germany to draw too closely to the Soviet Union and its allies.

Others see at least a possibility of redrawing the map of Europe laid down at Yalta by the anti-Axis Allies involving the gradual disappearance of the Iron Curtain. Yet others believe that these economic and political trends will sooner or later obliterate the differences in the underlying systems dividing Eastern and Western Europe and open the way for a greater European association embracing countries from the Atlantic to the Urals. Something along these lines was proposed by the former French President, Mr Valéry Giscard d'Estaing, in a speech to the Royal Institute for International Affairs in London on 12 July 1989.

Quite apart from the rapidly changing state of relations between East and West, there are profound global economic forces at work which both impact on the Europe of 1992 and which are, in their turn, affected by the way in which the European Community develops. For example the growing head-start of American and Japanese companies over their European rivals — particularly in terms of use of new technology and overall competitiveness — was a major reason why European industry came to support an initiative such as the barrier-free European market.

We shall examine later the arguments of the major European companies for the single market. But foremost among them is the belief that a large domestic market — combined with special support for industrial and specifically high-technology research, development and application — was vital if European corporations are to meet their US and Japanese competitors on world markets with any hope of survival.

But there is another side to the picture of the growing globalization of big business. That is the perceptible trend to visible, but more often invisible, protectionism in foreign trade.

The rights and wrongs of mutual charges of protectionism made against each other by the European Community, the United States and Japan, will be assessed later. But there is no doubt that in the eyes of some foreign governments, the 1992 project has at least, the potential to turn the EC into a protectionist 'fortress Europe'.

For example, the US Secretary of Commerce, Mr William Verity, wrote in *The Journal of Commerce* in October 1988 that 'The architects of the European 1992 programme — European government and industry leaders of vision ... seek to avoid a "fortress Europe". Unfortunately, [they] are under siege. There are indications that backsliding, narrow national interests and protectionism may grow as 1992 approaches'.

At the same time, and just a few days earlier, the Japanese Deputy Foreign Minister, Mr Michihiko Kunihiro, told the Royal Institute of International Affairs of his country's concern about the direction which the Europe of 1992 might take in handling its foreign trade relations. Referring to rumours that the EC might want to control Japanese car imports beyond 1992, Mr Kunihiro said 'Japan is seriously concerned over this issue and regards it as a test case of the EC's sincere commitment to truly opening its market to the outside world, in conformity with the rules of GATT'. These are charges which have been strongly denied by the European Commission. Meanwhile the Heads of State and Government of the Community, meeting in Rhodes in December 1988, declared that the Community had no interest or intention of 'turning in on itself'.

Meanwhile the European Community and Japan charge the American Congress with incipient protectionism, citing the adoption by Congress of the 1988 Trade Bill. This issue was the major cause of the partial failure of the GATT Uruguay Round mid-term review conference held in Montreal in December 1988. The Americans equally accuse the EC of protectionism, notably in refusing to agree to the complete abolition of all agricultural subsidies by the end of the century, and both the EC and the US criticize the continuing Japanese foreign trade surplus and the inadequate access of their exporters to the Japanese domestic market.

Clearly the world is a very different place than it was 10, let alone 20 or more years ago. Could it be that the world economy is breaking up into mutually suspicious and inward-looking global regions? How, in this uncertain future should the European Community balance the sometimes competing claims of global free trade — which have brought so many benefits to the consumer — with the preservation of key industry and employment?

It may be, though, that we are running too far ahead of ourselves. It is true that, at first sight, a European security policy, or a new relationship with Eastern Europe, or the future structure of the world economy are a very long way from the immediate bread-and-butter issues involved in eliminating political, fiscal, technical and other internal barriers to a single European market.

The reality, however, is that all of these issues are simultaneously technical and also highly political. This is particularly true of the relationship between the internal market as the future of the European Community monetary and social policy.

In the short run, this debate is likely to focus on three immediate sets of issues: the completion of the legislative programme to bring about the internal market by 1 January 1993; the proposed

European Community 'social dimension', and the Social Charter of Fundamental Rights in particular; and the conclusions of the Delors Committee report recommending a three-stage move to European monetary union.

This report was discussed by the European Council in Madrid in June 1989 and was broadly endorsed by the great majority of the participating Heads of State or Government. Indeed all 12 Member States committed themselves to begin the first stage of the three stages outlined in the Delors report, beginning in July 1990. This stage, which has so far been given no completion date, will concentrate primarily on improving cooperation on economic and monetary policy, but the three remaining countries whose currencies are still outside the EMS exchange-rate mechanism (the United Kingdom, Greece and Portugal) will be expected to become full members of the EMS during stage one.

At Madrid the UK Prime Minister, Mrs Thatcher, dropped a veiled hint that her government hoped to be in a position to 'peg' sterling within the EMS at some point after the start of stage one, but she expressed unqualified opposition to the more ambitious second and third stages of the Delors Committee recommendations for progress to monetary union. These begin a process of supranational scrutiny and eventually determination of key economic and monetary policies and envisage the establishment of a European Community central banking system and possibly a single currency.

In the autumn of 1989 intensive work was begun to prepare for stage one and to enable the convening of an inter-governmental conference, probably in September 1990, to consider possible changes to the Treaty of Rome. These changes will be necessary to implement many of the recommendations of the second and third stages of European monetary union (EMU).

The Delors Committee report has raised the debate among policy-makers, central bankers and financial experts about just how far and how fast the Community can move down the road to economic and monetary union. But at the time of writing the reluctance of the UK Government to sanction a Treaty change raises the possibility that the other EC governments who wish to press ahead might have to do so in a special agreement purely among themselves — much in the way that the European Monetary System was launched in 1979.

Thus far these debates have rarely involved the mass of so-called 'ordinary Europeans'. The fact is that EC debates are — in most Member States, most of the time — regarded as obscure, boring and even esoteric. As surveys conducted for the European Commission itself have confirmed, public opinion is increasingly indifferent, sceptical and disenchanted with the European Community as it has presented itself in recent years.

This is hardly surprising. The recent history of the Community has hardly always been inspiring. After the constitutional crisis in the mid-1960s, when General de Gaulle effectively instituted the right of national governments to veto EC legislation in cases where ministers could claim a vital national interest, the momentum for greater European unity, first triggered by the formation of the European Community in 1957, then slowed to a virtual halt.

The decade of the 1970s, did, it is true, see the enlargement of the original six-nation Community, first to nine and then to 12 Member States — with first Greece and then Portugal and Spain joining in the 1980s. The European Monetary System was introduced by the EC in 1979. It still lacks the full participation of four of the present 12 Member States — the United Kingdom, Greece, Portugal and Spain. However in June 1989 the Spanish Government announced that the peseta would join the EMS exchange-rate mechanism the following year.

These were, however, also years of global inflation and world-wide recession, the years of successive oil-price shocks, of a dangerously destabilized US dollar and of rising unemployment and widespread de-industrialization in the economies of the Community. Moreover the EC was grappling through this period with what appeared to be ever more intractable problems of its own domestic housekeeping.

The European Community budget, the priorities for EC expenditure and the uneven burden on Member States contributing to its revenue, were a bitter cause of strife during the late 1970s and early 1980s. The common agricultural policy — which accounted for more than 70% of EC spending — was widely discredited as food mountains and wine, milk and olive oil lakes built up, EC farm prices rose well above world levels and the Community found itself involved in ever greater commitments to subsidize the production and storage of unwanted food.

With national governments under growing financial and budgetary pressure at home, there was little support for any significant increase in the revenue ceiling permitted to the Community budget. As a result the Community was denied the resources it desperately needed for a growing number of non-agricultural policy objectives — notably regional and social development, research and development, and aid to associated Third World countries.

The internal wrangling over the EC budget and the reform of the CAP was further embittered by a protracted campaign by the United Kingdom to be compensated for part of its net contributions to the EC budget, the second largest of any Member State. This was a cause promoted with particular zeal by Mrs Thatcher and during those years several European Community summits were dominated to the exclusion of virtually every other issue by the explosive budget crisis.

It is hardly surprising, therefore, that the cause of European union languished during most of the 1970s. Periodic but largely ineffective efforts were made to encourage greater European monetary integration but these had little result until the establishment of the EMS.

At the end of 1975, the then Belgian Prime Minister, Mr Leo Tindemans, was invited to prepare a report on future steps to European economic and political union.[1] Mr Tindemans proposed a series of measures including greater foreign policy cooperation, increased regional and social development, policies to promote the rights of European citizens and a strengthening of the decision-making competence of the EC institutions. However, the report, while widely praised, was allowed to languish on the shelf; its provisions largely ignored.

---

[1]   The report by Mr Tindemans on the prospects for European union had been commissioned by the European Council held in Rome in 1974 and it was presented to the Brussels European Council in 1976. Its recommendations on monetary union closely followed an earlier report, the Werner report of 1969 and a more pessimistic view of the prospects for European union in the Marjolin report published in March 1975.

During this period it was largely due to the efforts of a relatively small number of European leaders — including the late Italian Commissioner and Communist Member of the European Parliament — Mr Altiero Spinelli — that the idea of European union was kept alive.[2] A small but vigorous European Federalist Movement remained an active pressure group but the tide seemed to be running in the opposite direction.

Indeed there were even predictions during these years that the internal stresses and strains were such that the European Community might fall apart. There was also a widespread belief that the European Community might be forced to adopt a 'two-tier' or 'two-speed' model.

The argument was advanced that the differences in the ability and readiness of different EC countries to integrate, both economically and politically, made it inevitable that some would move faster than others down the road to full European union. But the truth was that even in those Member States where there was the strongest tradition in favour of European union, governments were reluctant during these years to move ahead as rapidly as they had been in the early years of the Community.

For all these reasons the Community tended to move only at the pace of the slowest member of its caravan. Clearly unless this situation was resolved, any talk about putting the European union train back on the rails was completely utopian.

The new Commission which took office under the Presidency of the former French Minister for Finance, Mr Jacques Delors, in January 1985, understood that a radically new approach was necessary if momentum was to be put back into the process of European integration. The overriding objective of the Delors Commission was the successful adoption of the Single European Act (SEA).[3]

In the view of the Commission, the SEA would make possible a more effective decision-making process at Community level, it would set out the priority of completing the frontier and barrier-free European internal market, and by the same token would set a broad range of social and human objectives for the Community in the years ahead.

The most immediate task after the formal adoption of the Single European Act was to secure agreement among the 12 Member States on reform of the common agricultural policy and of the operating priorities for the Community's budget. In this way, the Commission hoped, it would be possible to settle once and for all the nagging and persistent conflict with the UK Government about the size of its net contributions to the EC budget.

At the same time budgetary reform, including both a switch of expenditure from agriculture to other priorities and an increase in budgetary revenues, would make possible a big increase in the Community's commitment to the poorer and less-developed regions and communities.

---

2   Mr Spinelli took the leading role in launching the 'Crocodile Club' of Members of the European Parliament who were committed to the goal of a fully fledged federal united States of Europe. The club was named after a well-known restaurant in Strasbourg where the MEPs first met — 'The Crocodile'. Another group of MEPs, on the initiative of the late Basil de Ferranti, formed the 'Kangaroo Group' to lobby for the removal of all internal borders in the Community. It was influential in winning support for the single European market.

3   I have made extensive use here and later of an excellent summary of the provisions of the single European market contained in *From Six to Twelve* by Frances Nicholson and Roger East, published by Longman, London, 1987.

Only once the poison of internal budget conflict was removed, could the Community look to the future and its longer-term goals.

As we shall see in the next chapter, the Commissioner appointed with responsibility for the internal market, Lord Cockfield, moved rapidly to introduce a programme of about 300 pieces of proposed legislation dealing with everything from frontier decontrol to the removal of technical barriers and the approximation of rates of value-added tax (VAT) and excise duties. The timing has proved right; the climate for such sweeping change had been prepared during the 1980s which saw a swing to free market and economic liberalization policies.

The process of passing the Single European Act was more complex and it met serious political resistance at several points. The Milan Summit of June 1985 approved, in principle, a paper setting out the proposals of the SEA; it was discussed at length in the special forum of an intergovernmental conference of Member States and finally approved at the Luxembourg European Council in December 1985.

However, its implementation was, even at that late stage, delayed by political problems in two Member States — Denmark and Ireland, where the Supreme Court ruled that Ireland's accession to the SEA had implications for the Irish Constitution. However the Danish and Irish electorate subsequently voted to endorse the SEA in referendums and the Act finally came into force on 1 July 1987. The Danes actually voted very quickly and were the first to ratify. The Irish, who were divided over the implications of the SEA for Ireland's neutrality, were the last.

Important though these developments were, little progress had been made in solving the immediate financial crisis facing the Community. Such was the over-expenditure on the CAP, that there were fears that the Community budget might be approaching technical bankruptcy.

It was in this highly charged atmosphere that the Heads of Government met in Copenhagen in December 1987 to negotiate a package agreement. This was intended to include an increase in the Community revenues (so-called 'own resources'), strict and statutory curbs over support for farm production, and a continuation of the arrangements under which the United Kingdom was rebated part of its gross contributions to the Community's budget.

That Summit ended in acrimonious failure — mainly over the details of the new agricultural disciplines needed to deter over-production — and the problem was handed over to the incoming German Presidency which took office in January 1987. The Federal Republic then called another emergency European Council in Brussels which, after two days and nights of intense bargaining, finally reached agreement.

For the first time legally enforceable controls were imposed on spending to support key agricultural products, laying the basis for a reduction in the share of the Community's finances devoted to the CAP from 70% to less than 60%. This in turn left a larger proportion of a bigger budget to be devoted to policies such as research and development and spending by the EC structural Funds, i.e. primarily on regional and social development which, it was agreed, would be doubled over the years to the end of 1992.

The Brussels Summit also gave explicit backing to the so-called 'Delors package'. This was a pro-gramme of action to assist the most vulnerable communities, regions and social groups and was directly drawn from the objectives set out in the Single European Act itself to create a citizens' Europe.[4]

At the heart of this package is the reform and doubling of the Community's structural Funds. These are the funds designed for regional development, social solidarity and programmes to assist workers and communities hit by agricultural and industrial restructuring.

The objective of the SEA, as the Commission put it at the time of the Brussels Summit, would be to ensure that the single European market brought wide benefits to all the peoples of the Community and specifically to help secure an improvement in the living and working condi-tions of Community citizens. This was particularly important for the poorer, mainly, though not exclusively, southern European countries some of whom had feared that the abolition of national controls would place their industries at risk to the more powerful economies of the north.

The success of the Brussels Summit transformed the political climate within the Community. For the first time in years there was a sense of forward movement and of optimism that the resolution of the Community's internal budgetary crisis would be followed by more rapid pro-gress both in completing the single market and accelerating economic integration.

There is little doubt that this sense of greater optimism was also fuelled by the remarkable economic recovery being experienced — in varying degrees — throughout the Community economies. Only a year earlier, in the aftermath of the dramatic international stock market crash of October 1987, there had been fears that the world economy, necessarily including the European Community, would slide into recession or even an outright economic slump.

Had that come to pass, EC governments might have been less ready to press ahead with measures of intra-Community liberalization and decontrol. It might also have led to closer ques-tioning of some of the economic assumptions behind the Commission's 1992 strategy which assume a benevolent interaction between microeconomic policies of liberalization and macroeconomic strategies of economic expansion.

It will be necessary to look more closely at these issues a little later, not least since no one can be sure whether an international economic recession is indefinitely postponed or only tem-porarily delayed — perhaps until the early 1990s. In the meantime, however, there has been far more concentration on the job-creating potential of the single market than the threat to employment which the abolition of obstacles to the market may involve in the more vulnerable industries and regions of the Community.

---

4 See *The social dimension of the internal market*, published by the European Commission, Brussels, September 1988.

Alongside all these developments, the Delors Commission has been waging a major struggle to convince Member States of the critical importance of a strengthening of the European Monetary System. In part this arises out of apprehension that full capital liberalization might not either happen, or might actually have serious disruptive economic effects, were it not to be accompanied by greater monetary cooperation and integration.

There is a second consideration, however. Throughout the previous decade the Community had become increasingly alarmed at the destabilizing economic effect of the unpredictable volatility of the United States dollar. The management of the US dollar as the linchpin currency in the world monetary system by successive Administrations in Washington had been a source of transatlantic friction.

Both internal factors, such as the need to ensure that all EC countries, participated in the new internal market on an equal footing, and the need to reduce the vulnerability of the EC currencies to external destabilization, argued for a much stronger EMS. The Delors Commission renewed, without tangible success, its pressure on the UK Government to allow sterling to become part of the fixed-exchange rate mechanism of the EMS.[5]

The UK Government was warned that it could not necessarily expect the full benefits of a liberalized European market in financial services, for example, if other Member States thought it was securing an unfair competitive advantage by refusing to fix the value of sterling against other EC currencies. The decision by Spain to become a full EMS member in 1990 left just the United Kingdom, Greece and Portugal to follow a little later.

The Commission realized that progress towards monetary integration would have to be accelerated even further. And in June 1988 it persuaded the Hanover European Council to ask a special Committee of central bank governors and monetary experts, chaired by President Delors himself, to study the next concrete steps towards greater monetary integration.

The terms of reference of the Committee permitted its members to study such radical options as the creation of a European Community central bank and even an eventual adoption of the European currency unit as a single EC money. The Committee was charged with reporting back with policy proposals to the Madrid Summit of Heads of State or Government which was held in June 1989.

As we have seen, the Committee agreed a three-stage plan for moving towards full economic and monetary union beginning in July 1990. A clear majority of the 12 Member States, at Madrid and subsequently, signalled their agreement in principle with the necessity of gradually transferring control of monetary and economic policy to the Community level — both through the Council of Financial and Economic Ministers and to a proposed European central banking system, roughly modelled on the pre-war United States Federal Reserve.

---

[5] At the time of writing — August 1989 — nine of the 12 European Community Member States had agreed that their currencies should be part of the fixed exchange-rate mechanism of the European Monetary System. Among those, the Italian lira was, however, permitted a greater margin in which it fluctuates against the other EMS currencies than the other participants. The currencies of the United Kingdom, Greece and Portugal remained outside the ERM, although all EC countries are members of the European Monetary System itself. In June 1989 the Spanish Government announced that the peseta would be pegged in the exchange-rate mechanism of the EMS from July 1990.

The prospect of such a development did provoke questioning in some quarters. The UK Government dismissed the prospect of a fully fledged central bank as 'out of the question' and there were also reservations among German central bankers. However the debate continued and in 1988 there appeared to be some signs of a convergence of views among the great majority of expert opinion in the Community in favour of a new move forward — perhaps in the first instance to a central banking body more like the US Federal Reserve, accountable in the first instance back to national central banks for its actions. Such a move would, however, require an amendment to the Treaty of Rome and plans were laid for an inter-governmental conference to be called, probably some time in 1990, to agree on such an amendment.

It was hardly surprising, in view of the sense of renewed progress in the Community, that its attraction for neighbouring European countries increased. The EFTA countries pressed for a European economic space linking EFTA and the EC. Nineteen eighty-eight also saw the mutual recognition agreement with Comecon and trade agreements with Czechoslovakia and Hungary.[6] Talks about equally far-reaching cooperation agreements got under way with the Soviet Union and Poland during 1989. There were also plans for rather more modest trade agreements — similar to that negotiated with Czechoslovakia — with Bulgaria and the German Democratic Republic.

Although the debates about the future of the European Community have, until this point, remained largely the property of a relatively small minority of decision-makers, opinion-formers and other professionals involved in EC affairs, there is every prospect of this changing. The European Parliament election campaign in June 1989 began to involve wider groups of citizens in discussing just these issues.

The European Parliament has, until recent years, somewhat languished among the Community decision-making institutions. Although directly elected since 1979, the Member States of the Community have always refused the European Parliament adequate direct power to amend, let alone determine, EC legislation.

In essence the European Parliament has been — at least until the SEA — little more than a consultative assembly. It is true that MEPs have had the power to sack the entire Commission or to reject — in its entirety — the annual EC budget.

However, in the nature of things, this has been an unusable weapon. On the other hand, MEPs had only very circumscribed rights to amend expenditure proposals contained in the budget, but they are powerless to hold the Council of Ministers — the real decision-making power centre in the Community — to account.

The situation of European Parliamentarians has been somewhat improved by the SEA, in so far as MEPs have been given a bigger say in amending EC legislation and therefore can hold

---

6   The agreement signed with Hungary covered areas of economic cooperation which were not included in the more limited trade agreement concluded, also in 1988, with Czechoslovakia. It was clear that the Community in determining the scope of agreements being negotiated with individual Comecon countries was influenced, among other matters, by the record of their governments in pursuing political liberalization and their observance of human rights.

up approval of laws of which they disapprove (as well as agreements with third countries). The first time these new powers were used to effect was in May 1989, when MEPs insisted on strengthening the terms of a draft directive adopted by the Council to control car exhaust emissions. However, in the view of the great mass of European Parliament Members and — increasingly — of public opinion, these reforms do not close the democratic deficit which exists in Community affairs. And the new post-SEA powers of MEPs can normally only be used with effect when the Council is badly divided and the Commission sides with the European Parliament.

What the SEA and the single European market is doing is to encourage what are essentially national political parties in the European Parliament to federate with like-minded parties and to offer the European electorate a clearer choice between the different 'Europes' on offer up to and beyond 1992. It is a process which showed every sign of acceleration following the election of a new European Parliament in June 1989.

In this sense we can begin to expect European Community politics to develop in a way which has never happened in the past. It is too soon to say whether this will lead to completely integrated Community-wide political parties, but the future federating of national political parties is already the subject of debate among European Parliamentarians.

The emergence of genuine European Community politics is bound to highlight the enormous gap between the concentration of executive power at EC level — as an inevitable by-product of the SEA and the single market — and the grossly inadequate powers of the elected representatives of the European Community voters. Public attention may focus increasingly on the other EC institutions, notably the Council, which does pass laws but in private and behind closed doors. There is a real question about the extent to which the Council, as such, is seriously accountable to anyone. National parliaments have some control over individual governments but lack the power to amend or reject decisions of the Council. And, as we have seen, the powers of the European Parliament in this respect are very restricted.

There is, it goes without saying, a danger that the current momentum behind economic and monetary integration, the abolition of all obstacles to the single market and the public acceptance of these trends — to say nothing of the more ambitious objective of a social Europe and ultimate political union — will be taken for granted. It would be foolish to imagine the process is — in the short run — either unproblematic, or in extreme circumstances, unstoppable.

The initial euphoria about the single market and the changes it will bring in its wake may not last. The detailed economic case for decontrol and liberalization is bound to come under ever greater public scrutiny in the Member States as the detailed legislation to make 1992 a reality comes under debate.

Already the trade-union movement is expressing concern in some countries about the dangers to employment and a lowering of social standards in the single market. Other interest groups including organizations representing disadvantaged social groups and regions which are either underdeveloped or suffering industrial decline, have also begun to ask searching questions about the entire 1992 project.

It is right, at this stage, therefore that we look in greater detail at the case made out for the single market and other measures which are meant to accompany it. It is also necessary to examine the specific proposals designed to bring the single market into being and to ask what their chances are of being fully adopted by the Council of Ministers and also adopted within the ambitious timetable set by the European Commission for the completion of the market by the end of 1992.

Chapter 2

The cost of 'non-Europe'

The dream of a European Community internal market is not new. The Single European Act — the first major amendment to the Treaty of Rome — which was finally adopted in 1987, aims to create an area without internal frontiers in which the free movement of goods and services, capital and persons is ensured. But this objective was at the very heart of the project which the six founding Member States set out when they signed the Treaty of Rome on 25 March 1957.

The six signatories made clear their intentions when they drew up the preamble to that Treaty. This stated that they planned to establish 'the foundations of an enduring and closer union between European peoples' by gradually eliminating the economic effects of their political frontiers.

The immediate target, in this context, was to be the 'elimination, as between Member States, of customs duties and of quantitive restrictions in regard to the importation and exportation of goods... and the establishment of a common customs tariff and a common commercial policy towards third countries'. Indeed this was effectively achieved, ahead of the original timetable, by the Six between 1968 and 1970.

However the Treaty went on to state — quite simply — the goal of the abolition, as between Member States, of the obstacles to the free movement of persons, services and capital. This was, however, to be understood as being intimately linked to the objective of economic prosperity, social justice (something about which the founders were singularly vague), balanced development, the creation of common social and other policies to help realize nothing less than full economic and — eventually — full political union.

It is easier in the 1980s to underestimate the wider political inspiration which drove many of the more narrowly economic objectives of the Community's founders. The preamble to the earlier European Coal and Steel Community — the forerunner to the EC — states baldly that they were 'resolved (to substitute for age-old rivalries the merging of essential interests; to create... the basis for a broader and deeper community among peoples long divided by blood, and, to lay the foundations for institutions which will give direction to a destiny henceforth shared'.

At the time these words were written the memory of the Second World War, and indeed the 1914-18 war, was still very vivid. There was a widespread conviction, particularly among many in the younger generation, that, without destroying the foundations of European economic nationalism, there would be the ever present danger of further European wars in the future. In particular there was a determination to remove, as far as possible, the economic basis for Franco-German conflict.

In retrospect there is something a little naïve about the belief, widespread at the time, that cultural and political foundations of nationalism would crumble at the mere sound of the trumpet of European free trade or even economic integration. The continuing potency of the nation State and the persistence of the politics of nationalism became evident again a decade after the foundation of the European Community during the challenge to the primacy of the EC institutions mounted by the French president, General de Gaulle.

It was not fully appreciated during those years that political integration would by no means automatically or naturally follow on the creation of an economic community. National Member States, even in the euphoria of the early years of the EC, were careful to keep effective control of the principal levers of political power — taxation and macroeconomic strategy, to say nothing of foreign and defence policy.

At the same time the Community was allowed to play only a modest role in determining wider social policies. For the average citizen of an EC country interested, for example, in health, education or pensions policy — the European Community came to seem a distant and marginal, if not irrelevant, centre of political decision-making. This contributed to a certain weakening of the identity of the European Community and the aspirations of ordinary Europeans.

There is little doubt that this as well as the recession following the two oil-shocks contributed to the decline of European fervour during the 1960s and 1970s when the goal of a federal Europe began to recede further and further. Moreover the European Community tended to attract attention mostly when there were internal squabbles over budgetary policy and over the shape and direction of the major Community spending commitment — the common agricultural policy. This further damaged the popular image of the Community.

Ironically while the Community tended to be blamed for the political failures in integration which were really the result of a highly defensive stand taken by the national Member States, it did not always get credit for the economic achievements of the years after 1957. Even so, there is no doubting the enormous transformation which has overcome the European Community economies in the past three decades. Since the signing of the Rome Treaty, trade between Member States has grown more than sevenfold while it has more than tripled with the rest of the world.

Production and living standards have more or less doubled since then — compared with a 70% increase in the United States. Now the credit for all of this cannot simply be taken by the progress in creating a customs union within the European Community. The years from 1957 to the early 1970s were years of sustained international boom, rapid technological change and remarkable growth in productivity.

The reduction and elimination of customs duties between EC Member States was crucial in fuelling the great boom and ensuring European industry's participation in it. Indirectly, it was responsible for the creation of a whole new generation of industries and enterprises.

Even so the arrested political development of the European Community was matched by an economic evolution which left it far short of the original goal of a barrier-free internal market. In many ways, as customs duties disappeared a variety of other — often less visible — barriers to cross-frontier trade began to appear.

The European Community economies remained impeded — to a large degree — by having not one but many different national markets. Of course the persistence and even the growth of a variety of governmental, fiscal and even physical barriers to trade in many cases can be explained by important national political and social pressures.

In many instances it was the understandable desire to protect jobs or industries whose continued existence was important either for national strategic reasons or because the jobs and prosperity of certain regions and communities crucially depended on them.

But at the same time, commercial Balkanization exacted a high cost in the lost opportunity of European industry to grow and develop in ways that could match the technological and commercial challenge of world competition. The lack of an internal market has contributed significantly to the uncompetitive cost structure of many European firms who have to compete in world markets.

It was never the case, however, that all the problems of European industry could be blamed on the lack of a single market. Other factors such as the tendency of European finance capital to take an unduly short-term view of risk, profit and innovation have played an important part in holding back investment in the technological development of sections of European industry.

The Commission, under the Presidency of Jacques Delors, which took office in January 1985 made the task of removing the physical, financial, political, technical and other barriers which enshrined the continued economic fragmentation of the Community its overriding political goal. The objective is to create a genuine single market of more than 320 million people, without barriers to trade or the free movement of capital, persons, services and trade. But, as we shall see, the significance of this historic exercise goes far beyond the purely commercial and economic levels.

It soon became apparent that meaningful progress towards a genuine internal market would only be possible as a result of a reform of the Community's decision-making institutions. The Delors Commission proposed the Single European Act, a series of amendments to the Treaty of Rome, the founding document of which enshrines the Constitution of the Community, to permit, among other things, more rapid decision-making.

The amendments were agreed after protracted negotiations by the Member States at the European Council held in Luxembourg in December 1985. At the time the Danish Government made its agreement conditional; subsequently the Irish Supreme Court ruled that the SEA had constitutional implications. However, these problems were resolved when in two referendums the Single European Act was approved by Danish and Irish voters.

The SEA could be summarized as follows.

Internal market. A deadline of 31 December 1992 was set for the establishment of the internal market as an 'area without frontiers in which the free movement of goods, persons, services and capital is ensured in accordance with the provisions of the Treaty.' Measures having 'as their object the establishment and operation of the internal market' were in general to be decided by a qualified majority in the Council instead of unanimously, as was previously the case.

Exceptions were to be made, however, for fiscal provisions including measures harmonizing indirect taxes and measures relating to the free movement of persons. Measures affecting health, safety, environmental protection and consumer protection were to be based on a high level of protection (in deference to countries such as Denmark and the Federal Republic of Germany so that their more stringent environment and safety standards would not be undermined by weaker provisions adopted by others).

At the same time the Commission or any Member State would be permitted to bring other Member States to the European Court of Justice for alleged abuse of such exemptions. The unanimity rule would remain for measures constituting a step back with regard to liberalization of capital movements, and also for matters relating to Community wide recognition of professional qualifications.

At UK and Irish insistence no steps to establish the internal market were to affect the right of Member States to maintain border controls on immigration from third countries and to combat terrorism, crime and the traffic in drugs. The French Government was reportedly unwilling to allow decisions by majority vote on matters concerning the liberalization of air and sea transport. A statement was also made by Greece that steps towards the establishment of the internal market have to 'take place in such a way as not to harm sensitive sectors of Member State economies.'

At the Luxembourg Summit meeting it was agreed that the European Commission would give an interim report on progress towards making the internal market a reality before 31 December 1988 and 31 December 1990. The 1988 report revealed that a little under 50% of the planned legislation had been agreed by the end of that year. A further report on areas still requiring harmonization is to be drawn up in 1992.

Monetary affairs. An article was added to the SEA stating that 'in order to ensure the convergence of economic and monetary policy which is necessary for the further development of the Community, Member States ... shall take into account the experience acquired in cooperation in the framework of the European Monetary System (EMS) and in developing the European currency unit (ecu), and shall respect existing powers in this field'. Moreover, the Treaty referred to a previous declaration of the European Council approving the objective of economic and monetary union going back to summits held in Paris in 1972, Bremen in 1978 and Brussels in 1979 setting up the EMS.

Economic and social cohesion. In order to promote its harmonious development overall, the Community was to develop and pursue its actions leading to strengthening its economic and social cohesion. In particular the Community was to aim to reduce the disparities between the various regions and backwardness of the least favoured regions (which the United Kingdom insisted include declining industrial regions).

Once the amended Treaty entered into force the Commission was to present proposals for the improvement of the existing structural Funds (the Guidance Section of the European Agricultural Guidance and Guarantee Fund and the European Social Fund), which were already considered to be adequately financed so far as budgetary resources permit.

The European Parliament. The institution of a procedure for cooperation with the European Parliament was agreed. For a decision whose adoption required the cooperation of the Parliament, a common position reached by qualified majority of the Council, based on a Commission proposal and an opinion of the European Parliament, has then to be sent back to the Parliament. If within three months the Parliament has approved the Council's decision or has failed to take a decision the act would be adopted. Within that period the Parliament could by an absolute majority of its constituent members either propose amendments to the Council's common position or reject it outright.

If a decision is rejected by the Parliament, the Council has to act unanimously on a second reading. Amendments proposed by the Parliament have to be re-examined by the Commission within one month, after which the Council has within three months either to accept the Commission's revised proposal by a qualified majority or to amend it by a unanimous decision. The position which would arise if the Parliament rejected the Council's common position at its second reading or if the Council failed to act within three months on a revised Commission proposal was left for further discussion between the three institutions but with the Council having the last say. This happened in 1988 when the European Parliament rejected a Commission proposal dealing with the health and safety of workers handling benzene.

Powers of the Commission. Certain increased and freshly defined powers for the Commission to implement agreed policy were also laid down.

Research and development. The SEA also aims to strengthen the scientific and technological base of European industry and to encourage it to become more competitive at international level. In pursuing these objectives in coordination with the activities in this field of Member States, the EC was (i) to implement research, demonstration and technological programmes by promoting cooperation with undertakings, research centres and universities; (ii) to promote cooperation with third countries and international organizations; (iii) to disseminate and optimize the use of the results of Community activities; and (iv) to stimulate the training and mobility of researchers in the Community. A multiannual framework programme and any bodies to execute EC research and development programmes were to be adopted unanimously by the Council but with detailed decisions being taken by a qualified majority.

Environment. Objectives set out in the SEA included (i) to preserve, protect and improve the quality of the environment; (ii) to contribute towards protecting human health; and (iii) to ensure the prudent and rational use of human resources. The priorities were to be preventive action, the rectification of environmental damage at source and the principle that the polluter should pay.

Social policy. Member States are enjoined to pay particular attention to encouraging improvements in the working environment, as regards the health and safety of workers, the objective being the harmonization of conditions in this area, while maintaining the improvements. Action should be taken by qualified majority in the Council but individual Member States were not to be prevented from introducing more stringent measures. The Commission was also invited to endeavour to develop the dialogue between management and labour at the European level, which could place a reserve on this section initially. As a result legislation affecting, for example, workers' rights is still subject to national veto.

Political cooperation. A provisional text was agreed which largely codified existing practice regarding foreign policy cooperation — the political cooperation process. Member States agreed to inform and consult each other on any policy matters of general interest so as to ensure that their combined influence is exercised as effectively as possible.

Governments are expected to turn common principles and objectives into common policies and to adopt common positions in international institutions and conferences. Political dialogue with third countries and regional groupings and liaison between foreign embassies of Member States was to be stepped up.

In a development with major implications for the future, the SEA stipulates that closer cooperation on questions of European security would contribute in an essential way to the development of a European external identity while in no way weakening the role of NATO or the Western European Union to which most, though not all, Member States belong. The European Parliament is to be more closely associated with discussion of foreign and security policy and a secretariat to coordinate work on political cooperation has been established in Brussels.[1]

A word should be said about the voting system in the Council of Ministers. Each Member State is allotted a number of votes in accordance with its size which, for the present 12 Member States totals 76. A qualified majority is a decision which attracts a minimum of 54 votes. The votes allotted to each Member State were as follows: Belgium (5), Denmark (3), France (10), Greece (5), Ireland (3), Italy (10), Luxembourg (2), the Netherlands (5), Portugal (5), Spain (8), the United Kingdom (10) and the FR of Germany (10).[2]

It would be wrong to suggest that there are no sectors of the European Community economies which are not already highly competitive. But the facts outlined in the Cecchini report prepared for the European Commission on the cost of 'non-Europe' have not been subject to any serious intellectual challenge.

---

[1] The questions raised by European political cooperation, particularly in the field of security policy, are examined later.
[2] A similarly proportional system is used to allocate senior posts in the Community institutions, including the Commission, among nationals of the 12 Member States.

The report estimates that the cost of maintaining the present array of barriers to free trade and free movement of capital and people is more than ECU 200 billion; or, to put it the other way round, the Cecchini report claims that this could be the potential direct economic benefit from eliminating barriers and creating a single market.

The argument in support of this case is relatively simple. In the words of the Cecchini report 'The release of these constraints will trigger a supply-side shock to the European economy as a whole. The name of the shock is European market integration. Costs will come down. Prices will follow as business, under the pressure of new rivals on previously protected markets, is forced to develop fresh responses to a novel and permanently changing situation'.

The benefits from European Community market integration, the Commission believes, will be significant. The Cecchini report concluded that the elimination of the barriers would, over a period of years, add a cumulative 4.5% to the Community's gross domestic product and would, simultaneously, deflate consumer prices by an average of 6.1%.

Moreover the report calculated that the process of market liberalization would improve the over-balance of public finances in the EC by an average equivalent to 2.2% of GDP and would boost the external trade balance of the Community by about 1% of GDP. The direct boost to employment is translated in terms of an additional 1.8 million new jobs making it possible to reduce current levels of unemployment by about 1.5 percentage points.

The predictions do not end there. At the heart of the economic case for the single market is the assumption that the improvements in output, competitiveness and inflation will create space for more vigorous government economic action to boost growth. This, the Cecchini report hopes, would be achieved as a result of a concerted European Community 'better my neighbour' reflation strategy.

The overall result, the report concludes, could be to boost the Community's GDP by some 7% in the medium term and this could generate 5 million new jobs without any underlying growth in the rate of inflation. Finally, it is suggested, a market integration plus reflation strategy would still leave Member State governments, on average, with a budgetary gain equal to about 0.7% of GDP — enough, they hope, to reassure even the most financially orthodox of national administrations.

All of this assumes that the national frontier, tax and other barriers to a single market are as costly as the proponents of market integration believe. But just what is the present state of affairs in the European Community? Is the case of the integrationists unanswerable or even as solid as it looks?

At first sight it may seem strange to emphasize the continued fragmentation of the European Community. Europe — indeed the world — has shrunk and is made smaller with every new innovation in technology, communication and popular travel.

The average European travels abroad now to an extent which would have seemed impossible little more than a generation ago. People know more about how their neighbours live and work and about how much they have in common. Of course, television has also played a significant part in altering popular consciousness of the world in which we live and giving the people the capacity to vault over national frontiers and over the prejudices and ignorance about the outside world which clouded the judgments of previous generations.

Meanwhile a visit to any supermarket in any country of the European Community will confirm the enormous changes which have taken place in consumer tastes. On the shelves of our shops and stores are to be found goods from all over Europe, indeed all over the world.

Moreover, and despite the direct and indirect barriers to free trade and the free movement of capital, there has been a striking internationalization of most if not all the production industries in the European Community. The major European (and international) corporations have branches and subsidiaries in the majority of EC countries. In some cases, such as pharmaceuticals, this is precisely because of local investment requirements in 'non-Europe'.

Some actually organize their production on a transnational basis. A car manufactured by, say, the Ford motor company in Dagenham near London, consists of components and whole sections made in half a dozen different plants in different countries.

So we can conclude that, despite the fragmented European market, a degree of international integration of production and distribution has already occurred. The case made by the European Commission is that it is hopelessly inadequate when measured against the size of the domestic market base of, for example, the United States.

But it should be pointed out that the absence of a continental scale domestic market base has not been a noticeable constraint on the development of the powerful Japanese industrial machine. Neither should it be forgotten, as we shall see later, that there are bound to be losers as well as winners in the process of removing barriers and other curbs on the growth of an integrated European market.

But what are the more or less direct barriers which fragment the EC market at present? They fall into three main types which should be looked at separately: (i) technical barriers — resulting in the main from the profusion of different national product standards, technical regulations, conflicting business laws and nationally protected public procurement markets; (ii) fiscal barriers — notably different rates of VAT and customs and excise duties; and (iii) physical, or frontier, controls.

When the Commission's 1985 White Paper was presented, it was clear that while, by then, most of the policy-makers in Brussels and the experts elsewhere were aware that the lack of an internal market was costing *something,* no proper assessment of economic analysis had ever been made to the cost of a 'non-Europe'. It might be thought unusual to draw up detailed policy proposals and then assess fully the original justification and the potential effect of those proposals.

The fact remains that the evidence collected up to the point, in 1986, when Lord Cockfield asked Paolo Cecchini to organize a comprehensive study consisted of very partial assessments drawn up by relevant Directorates-General of the Commission or by Members of the European Parliament. All suffered from either their extremely sectoral nature, or from a lack of time or resources which led to inevitably insubstantiated extrapolations being made from the small amount of data available.

In presenting the case for the completion of the internal market, therefore, the Commission was forced to rely on these early and incomplete estimates, which left it open to challenge on several grounds.

But once the decision was made to compensate for this lack of firm evidence, the study undertaken by Cecchini was given very widespread power and resources to call in large teams of experts in every field covering the internal market. A total of 24 research teams, led by academics, consultancy companies or national institutes, made their contribution to the study, which in the end amounted to some 20 000 pages of published material, reproduced in several volumes. Of course, the overall conclusion of the study was that the process is indeed worthwhile, but as we have seen, the research undertaken also revealed many factors which show that the full benefits are achievable only on certain conditions.

For the purposes of the economic analysis undertaken by Cecchini and his team of experts, the three types of market barriers which were identified in the 1985 White Paper were regrouped into five categories: tariffs, quantitative restrictions (quotas), cost-increasing barriers, market-entry restrictions, and market-distorting subsidies and practices.

By and large, *tariffs* have been all but eliminated within the Community, and those which remain, especially in the industrial sector, between Spain and Portugal and the 'old' Community are set to disappear, as part of the transition arrangements, by 1992. Otherwise, for the moment, tariffs in the form of Monetary compensatory amounts (MCAs) — the complex system of cross-border taxes and subsidies in the agricultural sector which attempt to neutralize currency differences between the Member States in order to provide common prices to farmers throughout the Community — are the only ones to persist. The gradual phasing out of MCAs has also been agreed by the Member States over the period up to 1992. The conclusion reached by the Cecchini report is that, of all the types of market barrier, tariffs are amongst the least significant when assessing the cost of 'non-Europe'. Although they impose a cost on consumers, both by increasing the cost of imports and by allowing a degree of inefficiency or extra profits for domestic producers.

The second type of market barrier, *quantitative restrictions,* have also been considerably reduced within the Community, but some quotas persist, and have an effect similar to restrictions on trade. In the production sector, for example, quotas have existed until recently on steel output, and are a key feature in the agricultural sector as the Community continues its efforts to reduce production of farm products in surplus. And in the service sector, effective quotas in the form of licensing and regulatory systems still apply in air and road transport. Finally, some Member States continue to impose national quotas on imports — notably of cars and textiles — from non-EC countries, and the Treaty allows, through use of Article 115, occasional restrictions to be placed on the free movement of imports from non-EC countries to provide temporary protection for national markets.

In contrast to formal tariffs, such quantitative restrictions do not bring in any revenue for the Community budget, and Cecchini points out that it is the exporter who benefits instead, by way of increased profits. In addition, he stresses that the restrictions mean there is no fixed ceiling on the cost of protection afforded to domestic producers. That cost is often passed on to the consumer.

The effect of production quotas is similar, with the further disadvantage of limiting competition within Member States and risking greater inefficiency, the report concludes.

The first of the two types of market barrier on which the White Paper concentrates is that of so-called 'cost-increasing barriers,' which include delays at frontiers and technical regulations. The delays at frontiers are caused by the need to administer a wide range of regulations, such as assessing or collecting value-added tax or excise duty, collecting statistics, or checking that the vehicles and goods conform with various technical rules. Similar economic effects are caused by the costs of respecting technical rules in the fields of production, packaging and marketing of goods. The overall impact of these barriers is to put up the cost of goods to consumers, says the Commission, and allow a corresponding margin or inefficiency and/or extra profits for domestic producers. The supplier in another Member State has to bear the extra costs, and since no tariffs are payable, the unfavourable impact on consumers is not offset.

The other main type of market barrier which qualifies for a considerable number of proposals in the White Paper concern *market-entry restrictions*, which the Commission agrees can be difficult to distinguish from the cost-increasing barriers. This category includes government procurement restrictions, the right of establishment for various service industries and professions, restrictions in some service sectors (such as insurance or electricity) which prevent or limit direct trading across frontiers, and restrictions on entry into some regulated markets (such as civil aviation). The right of establishment is in the Treaty but national regulations frequently ensure that this right is more theoretical than practical. These types of restrictions, says the Commission, exclude competition, whereas cost-increasing barriers still allow competition to work. Economic analysis of the impact of market-entry restrictions shows that this varies according to the type — where the entry barrier is absolute, the effect is equivalent to a zero quota; in cases of exchange controls on capital movements and establishment in certain sectors, the Commission concludes, 'the restriction may be overcome, but with a certain cost of delay for the entrants'.

The final type of market barrier concerns *market-distorting subsidies and practices*, most of which can already be dealt with by the Commission under competition powers, either in respect of aid granted by the State or other authority, or in cases of abuses committed by private companies. Other areas which could be dealt with in the future include, for example, merger control, but the main concern of the Commission's White Paper is the full application of the existing rules. The Commission adds that price controls and specific taxes may also distort some markets in ways relevant to the internal market programme.

The economic impact of such subsidies or practices act as a competitive disadvantage to foreign suppliers, and as a protection of inefficiency for domestic suppliers, the Commission has concluded. The consequences for the consumer are higher taxes, rather than higher prices.

As well as commissioning a series of studies on specific sectors and problems relating to the cost of 'non-Europe', Cecchini's research involved undertaking a large-scale survey of industry's attitudes and perceptions of the issue.[3]

---

3   It is fair to say that the central conclusions drawn in the Cecchini report about industry's attitudes to the cost of 'non-Europe' are borne out by most other studies of the issue.

Many of the conclusions drawn by him, and in policy terms by the Commission, are based on the results of that survey. Using a variety of intermediaries in the Member States, including statistical institutes, business confederations, market research bureaux and government agencies, the team sent out detailed questionnaires to some 20 000 industrialists and received 11 000 replies. Clearly, the conclusions which lead from the survey are based on expression of opinion (in the style of 'How desirable would you consider for your company the need to remove the following barriers to a completely open common market in the European Community?', followed by a list of the types of barriers and boxes to tick ranging from very important to 'We are satisfied with the present situation') and more precise estimates of the cost of 'non-Europe' are based on clear empirical evidence gathered during market surveys in the various areas and sectors.

The team leader for the industry survey makes the point clearly himself when he says 'the survey's results need to be viewed circumspectly. They are only one element, albeit an important one, to be factored into the establishment of public policy priorities ... it is nevertheless essential for economic policy managers to know the expectations, hopes and fears which companies associate with the European market integration. In the end, these attitudes and expectations — even if not always well founded — largely determine companies' decisions concerning investment, research, product strategy etc., and for that reason are to some extent self-fulfilling'.[4]

As part of the questionnaire, respondents were asked to make quantified assessments of the benefits which would accrue to their company as a result of a series of changes leading to the completion of the internal market, and these figures — suitably weighted to give a more accurate picture — have been used widely to draw up the Commission's estimates of the cost savings which the removal of intra-EC barriers would allow, together with the possible impact on sales and business strategies. In this area, the sort of question asked of industry was, for example, 'By about what percentage would your total order volume be higher or lower than without the completion of the internal market?', together with an invitation to assess, on a cost per unit basis, 'How large a change would you expect for your company's typical or average unit?'

But what does emerge quite clearly is a picture of which barriers the industrialists believe are costing them hard cash, and an order of importance of how serious the various barriers are to their business. In this league table, the industrialists give about equal weight to technical standards and regulations and administrative barriers, followed by frontier formalities, freight transport regulations, and, again with similar weight, differences in value-added tax between Member States, control on capital markets, restrictions of government procurement, and the implementation of Community law.

The research obviously produced several variables in this league table, mainly by Member State, type of business, and size of form, and the Commission concludes that 'this suggests that a comprehensive programme of actions, implying many detailed measures, may indeed be necessary to convince industrialists to base their business strategies on the assumption of an integrated European market'. Drawing on the results of the industrialists' questionnaire and research carried out in the field by other teams, an estimate of the economic cost of each broad category of barrier was drawn up by the experts.

---

[1] Cecchini, op. cit.

The assessment made of *customs procedures* covered the costs arising from frontier stops either at internal Community borders or inland, together with the related administrative costs borne inland by companies and the public authorities. Included in this category are the checks made necessary by differences in VAT and excise, the application of MCAs, differences in national public health standards, regulations covering vehicles and their drivers, the gathering of statistics, and the enforcement of remaining bilateral trade quotas with non-EC countries.

Grouping together the various effects that these formalities have on exporting and importing firms, and on the public administrations obliged to maintain staff and services directly involved in implementing the formalities, accountants Ernst and Whinney estimated that the total *direct* cost of customs formalities is between ECU 8.4 billion and 9.3 billion a year. On the basis of overall trade between the Member States of some ECU 500 billion a year, it is estimated that the direct cost of the formalities could represent between 1.7 and 1.9% of total intra-Community trade.[5]

Broken down, the estimated cost to firms of the administration involved is put at some ECU 7.5 billion, the costs of frontier delays at between ECU 400 million and 800 million, and administrative costs to public authorities at between ECU 500 million and ECU 1 billion. And once again, significant differences were found between the Member States — the Benelux countries compared with Italy, for example — and between import and export costs. In addition, the survey found that the costs were markedly higher for smaller companies, as larger firms are more able either to absorb the costs, or to make special arrangements to overcome at least part of the obstacle of formalities.

Even when border controls are eliminated, freight drivers will still take compulsory rest periods — an obligation which will remain even when the frontiers themselves disappear. As a result the estimates made of cost incurred by the road-haulage sector varies between the ECU 0.4 billion and 0.8 billion mark on the assumption that only a 50% saving can be achieved. The estimate made of the indirect costs to industry and business of the maintenance of customs procedures is, the Commission admits, much more difficult to assess precisely. But on the basis of the 'simple and very partial' attempt made by Ernst and Whinney to evaluate the possible extent to which companies might expand their trading activities, an increase of 1% for importers and 3.2% for exporters was predicted if customs formalities were abolished. Cecchini points out, however that these results take no account of possible increases in trade by firms which are not engaged in trade at present, or the increase in trade between border regions by small traders or individuals.[6]

Moving on to *technical regulations,* the Commission admits that, owing to the existing number of such regulations — up to 100 000, it has been estimated — and the fact that the field is continuing to grow as technology advances and health, safety and consumer protection concerns multiply, a proper quantification of the costs to business and industry is impossible. Amongst the vast range of such barriers, many of which are there for completely legitimate reasons — such as quality, safety or compatibility between similar products — are standards set by industry

5   See 'The cost of "non-Europe". Customs barriers', Ernst and Whinney, London 1988.
6   Cecchini, op. cit.

itself or by national authorities or standards organizations like the Federal Republic of Germany's DIN, the UK's BSI, France's Afnor and others.

In general terms, the estimate of the economic costs which stem from the technical regulations depends on a set of variables relating to business attitudes, the type of product involved and, especially, general economic behaviour.

But the results of these regulations are stated to be, for companies, duplication in their research and development costs, the need to operate separate production lines for different markets, increased inventory and distribution costs, and competitive weaknesses on world markets as a result of the small national market base. The second major losers are the public authorities, for whom the duplication of testing and certification result in extra costs. Finally, the consumer and taxpayer loses out through the higher prices and taxes which result from the direct costs of producers and public authorities, and indirect losses 'often perhaps larger in size' stemming from the reduced competition and rationalizing in production and marketing structures.

In addition, the Cecchini report attempted, on the basis of the survey of industrialists, to rank technical barriers for the different branches of industry. This ranking shows that such barriers are an important problem in the fields of electrical engineering, mechanical engineering, the chemical industry, the food and tobacco sector, and the precision and medical equipment sector.

Turning to barriers caused through public procurement policies, the Commission estimates that over ECU 20 billion could be saved if public procurement policies were fully liberalized. This category includes all purchases of goods and services by the various levels of government and by the range of public enterprises (which the Commission defines as enterprises that benefit from a monopoly, franchise or special status in their provision of public services, such as energy, post and telecommunications or the railways). The value of such purchases in 1986 throughout the Community has been put at ECU 530 billion, or 15% of gross domestic product, a figure which situates the importance of the sector as part of overall economic activity.

Apart from motor vehicles, it is estimated that some 85% of capital expenditure in this sector is concentrated on transport equipment and on construction and civil engineering.

And the facts are that, at present, only about 2% of public supply contracts and 2% of public construction contracts are fully open to competition between firms in the different Member States, based on the award of contracts. In estimating the potential cost benefits of liberalization in this area, a first step taken by management consultants W. S. Atkins[7] was to assess the result of public purchasing bodies selecting the most competitive supplier. At once the direct economic effects of this phenomenon were drawn from these assessments, further calculations were made of the indirect consequences that liberalized public procurement might have, in cost terms and in terms of the practical effects on the firms involved.

Domestic suppliers would be obliged to drop their prices to the level of their competitors in other Member States, which should result in a reduction or even elimination of inefficiency (defined by the Commission as the 'poor internal allocation of *resources* — human, physical and financial') in their production. Later, an expected reduction in the number of suppliers would result

---

[7]   This point is echoed in a study entitled '1992 — the impact', published by Allen and Overy, London, September 1988.

in better capacity utilization in those which remain. Finally, the assumption is that long-term restructuring in the small number of industries involved would be worth some ECU 7.2 billion in the Community as a whole (on the basis of 1984 figures).

The overall costs of ECU 20 billion are arrived at by adding together the effects of choosing the most competitive supplier (ECU 4.4 billion), increased competition (ECU 2.3 billion) and restructuring (ECU 7.2 billion), and topping the total up with an estimate of potential savings in the defence sector (ECU 4 billion on annual public purchasing of about ECU 30 billion). Finally, the 1984 figures have been extrapolated for 1987, on the basis of a constant proportion of GDP.

The wide difference in indirect tax rates — fiscal frontiers — combined with the consequential need to de-tax intra-Community trade when it is exported, and tax it when it is imported, 'in effect divides the Community into 12 self-contained fiscal compartments', says the Commission. The proposals made to approximate VAT rates and excise duties throughout the Community are not aimed at achieving an 'optimum tax system for the Community', adds the Commission, but rather to do enough to make it possible to abolish the frontiers between Member States.

The proposals themselves (dealt with in the following chapter) are, says the Commission, 'designed to limit as far as possible, given the initial situation, the budgetary consequences for the maximum number of Member States'. But as the Member States have been given the right to decide, in the period up to the end of 1992, how to make the proposed tax changes, no attempt has been made to assess *all* the economic consequences. No specific study on the effects of removing fiscal barriers to trade was undertaken as part of the Cecchini report, although conclusions were drawn from the elements of other studies which included this aspect.

Overall, while it is difficult to separate the benefits of removing fiscal barriers from the advantages of scrapping other types of obstacles to trade, the Cecchini report economic experts have tried to describe the potential benefits. As has been seen, the first advantage would be the savings achieved as frontier controls and the administrative costs relating to these controls are removed. The second benefit would come from the price and cost reductions which are expected to result from increased competition.

The competitive effects are expected to arise from, in the first place, greater cross-border purchases — especially by individuals — which would force uncompetitive prices down. Other advantages would be a reduction in price distortions leading directly from different rates of tax — on pre-tax prices of cars on the different national markets, for example — and the greater credibility and predictability of indirect taxation policy for firms and individuals. Aside from the competitive advantages and the savings achieved by removing border controls, the Commission believes that 'the psychological impact alone of it becoming possible for both enterprises and individuals to drive across frontiers with absolutely no hindrance, can hardly be underestimated'.

While the Commission, for evident reasons, continues to stress that *all* the measures they have proposed must be adopted in order to achieve the full benefits of the completion of the internal market, it is clear that a number of the potential advantages are assumed by the analysts, judging by the results of even this quite extensive research. For the Commission, the conclusion to be drawn, apart from the importance of suitable economic conditions, is that its existing or potential powers in the area of competition policy must be applied fully. Overall, the Commission's economists assess the general benefits of removing barriers to be, first, a significant reduction in costs due to a better exploitation of several kinds of economies of scale associated with the size of production units and enterprises; second, an improved efficiency in enterprises, a rationalization of industrial structures and a setting of prices closer to costs of production, all resulting from more competitive markets; third, adjustments between industries on the basis of fuller play of comparative advantages in an integrated market; and finally, a flow of innovations, new processes and new products, stimulated by the dynamics of the internal market.

And, even though the Cecchini exercise is the most comprehensive attempt yet made to assess the cost of 'non-Europe' and of the potential benefits of the process now under way to complete the internal market, a very careful analysis needs to be made of the various models and assumptions made — not for their nature or legitimacy, but for the conclusions which have been and will be drawn from the evidence presented. As the Commission's own economic experts point out in their study, 'any estimates of the effects of a complex action like completing the internal market can only be regarded as very approximate. Apart from being subject to a number of policy conditions, such estimates are extremely difficult to make, especially as regards some of the more speculative and long-term effects'. As we shall see, judgments on these issues are likely to form part of the debate now taking place on the wider economic and social goals of the new Europe.

Chapter 3

Relaunching Europe

'The European Council considers that this major objective set by the Single Act has now reached the point where it is irreversible, a fact accepted by those engaged in economic and social life', said the EC's Heads of State or Government at their European Summit in Hanover in June 1988.

From the total of 285 separate proposals put forward by the Commission in the programme to complete the single market, the score achieved following the last Internal Market Council, on 22 June 1988, was 91 adopted (including six partial adoptions), a further 107 proposals on the Council table, and 87 still to be put forward by the Commission.[1] By the end of that year some 47% of the Commission's proposals had been effectively agreed by the Council.

On the basis of its own timetable, established first with the White Paper in 1985, the Commission decided in 1987 that, in order to meet the 1992 deadline, work would have to be speeded up considerably. Accordingly, the Commission has set itself the target of tabling 90% of the remaining White Paper proposals by the end of 1988, giving a full four years for their adoption and implementation. In spite of some acceleration in the Council's process of adoption, it is clear that a further and major effort will be needed on all sides. A key advantage in this respect is the psychological impact of having set 1992 firmly in the minds of even the less interested in the Community — which has the effect either of concentrating efforts or of instilling a sense of panic of being left behind compared with competitors. However, a major test will come over the Commission's continued — and understandable — assertion that it is necessary to adopt every one of its proposals in order to draw the full advantage of a single market. As we will see, a crucial challenge has already been made with regard to the plan to approximate VAT and exise duties throughout the EC. But for the Commission, a single reason for maintaining controls at internal frontiers would defeat the whole exercise.

The 1985 White Paper, drawn up in direct response to a request from the Heads of State and Government, provided the first comprehensive programme of measures thought necessary to complete the EC's internal market. The philosophy behind its approach was to recognize the

---

[1] In November 1988 it was predicted that by the end of that year, at the point of the Commission's mid-term review of progress in implementing the measures to realize the single market, some 90% of the 279 planned pieces of legislation would have been tabled and some 45% would either have been finally agreed or agreed in principle by the Council of Ministers.

interrelationship between the various barriers to trade within the Community — confirmed by the results of the studies carried out on the costs of 'non-Europe' — and to set out a clear timetable for the years up to 1992.[2] And amongst the 299 proposals originally put forward (20 have since been withdrawn), plans to give many million EC citizens the right to offer professional services in another Member State carry equal weight with measures to harmonize the certification of seeds throughout the Community. The proposals have been grouped into three broad categories: (i) the removal of physical barriers; (ii) the removal of technical barriers; and (iii) the removal of fiscal barriers. The description which follows keeps to these categories.

The physical barriers at internal frontiers in the Community can be a source of delay for goods travelling through several Member States (up to ECU 800 million extra cost to business if the Commission's estimate is accurate) but they are also the most visible manifestation of a Community divided into separate Member States. The Commission's proposals therefore call for the total removal of these frontiers, by doing away with the need to carry out controls motivated by fiscal, commercial, economic, health, veterinary, phytosanitary, statistical and policing considerations.

The controls carried out on people at internal frontiers, either systematic or at random, remain essentially for two purposes: immigration control and for tax reasons. As things stand, these controls can vary wildly around the Community, and even crossing the same border in one or another form of transport can affect the kind of checks carried out on travellers. The removal of the need to carry out immigration checks, the Commission believes, will require measures which will ensure that satisfactory controls can still be made to prevent crime and to deal with the movements of non-EC travellers. It is argued that policing can be carried out satisfactorily within Member States themselves, without the need for checks at the internal frontiers, while immigration controls for non-EC citizens should be carried out only at the Community's external borders — airports, sea ports and land frontiers with third countries. The Commission does not accept that ports and airports are necessary external frontiers. A freight between two countries' cities would be an internal freight for frontier purposes.

Clearly, while increased cooperation between the police forces of the different Member States will contribute to more effective controls on Community citizens as they travel from one country to another, this raises complicated questions about individual freedom. The tendency towards an EC-wide identity card is inevitable, but will be resisted in the United Kingdom and Ireland where ID cards are not the chosen means of control of the population by the authorities.

Checks carried out for tax reasons would largely disappear if the Commission's proposals to approximate VAT rates, to harmonize excise duties and to set up a clearing-house system were to be taken up by the Member States. These proposals are described further on in this chapter.

The complex series of checks on goods crossing the internal EC frontiers are proving as stubborn as fiscal checks and checks on people. The Commission's proposals lie in three main areas: abolishing some of the formalities, simplifying others, and transferring those which remain away from frontiers. A major step will be to do away with the need for systematic checks on

---

2   The White Paper was subsequently referred to a special intergovernmental conference of the 12 Community Member States, prior to the adoption of the Single European Act in December 1985.

vehicles crossing borders, checks which result in some notorious bottlenecks at certain frontiers — on either side of the Channel and on the border with Italy, for example. The Commission's plan foresees measures to considerably reduce the number and type of controls carried out at borders, by the end of 1988, while other moves are planned to completely eliminate the remaining controls, carried out internally, by 1992.

As growing use is made of the Single administrative document (SAD) to replace the plethora of documentation formerly required for the import and export of goods, new systems allowing the information carried on the SAD to be computerized can be introduced. But there are problems here which have already emerged, as several rival systems — even within Member States — are competing to become the Community's standard equipment. Nevertheless, the achievement of distilling hundreds of separate documents and requirements down to a SAD with 70 basic questions should not be underestimated. Aside from purely administrative checks, the fundamental reasons for continuing controls on goods at frontiers are various rules and regulations which have not been sufficiently harmonized at EC level.

In the field of transport itself, remaining restrictions on the number of licences granted to hauliers to undertake international transport have imposed an artificial limit on the road-haulage sector. As well as constraining free trade and competition, these quotas are an additional reason for maintaining controls at the frontier. It has been estimated that as many as 50% of the lorries crossing internal EC borders are in fact empty, largely as a result either of the quotas or of a continuing ban on the practice of cabotage — allowing haulage firms to ply their trade in a third Member State even if their original trip involves taking goods between Country A and Country B.

The EC's Transport Ministers now seem well on the way to abolishing these artificial restrictions by 1992, in addition to the physical checks on the design and roadworthiness of vehicles crossing borders. And provided that hauliers can prove their ability and business reliability, restriction on access to the haulage sector anywhere in the Community has now been removed.

It should be mentioned, as the Commission has itself recognized, that the full estimated cost of delays at frontiers cannot be recovered even if the borders themselves disappear, since social regulations, requiring rest periods to be taken by drivers, will continue to operate. Instead of taking those rest periods, as is often the case, at frontiers where delays are predictable, the drivers will have to take them elsewhere on the route.

The border checks necessary in the pursuance of various Community commercial or industrial policies are also the subject of separate Commission proposals, though not necessarily strictly within the White Paper. The controls necessary on steel products, for example, are set to disappear with the ending of the production quotas introduced in the early 1980s to help deal with the 'state of manifest crisis' in the EC's steel sector. In the area of trade policy, especially on textiles, the Commission foresees alternative ways of carrying out controls on goods subject to limited free movement around the Community. And the gathering of statistics for a whole range of purposes, such as measuring trade performance, will need to be moved away from the frontier. Finally, a system of mutual recognition of checks at origin in the field of plant and animal health, combined with further checks at destination, will need to be brought in to replace yet another important reason for holding up consignments at frontiers between the Member States.

'The long-term objective', says the Commission about this latter field, 'is to raise the health standards of all Member States to the highest levels so there is no need for any restriction on trade.'

The whole area of removing technical barriers to trade within the European Community is dominated by the complexity of the task. As we have seen, the estimated 100 000 different technical regulations and standards currently in operation in the EC are rated by the industrialists to be the single most important category of trade barrier.

Although the general justification for maintaining such standards have involved health, safety or environmental considerations, some have, on occasion, been used to provide artificial protection for markets or industries, and have certainly added billions to the costs of companies throughout the Community. The barriers range from different construction norms for a wide range of products to the German purity laws for beer.

To respond to the challenge of making substantial inroads into this layer of unnecessary national legislation, the Commission has now adopted a significant range of policy instruments. First, the principle of mutual recognition of national regulations, established by the 1979 Cassis de Dijon case in the Court of Justice,[3] has done a great deal to remove the need for harmonization of regulations. Community-wide. As a by-product of a reduced level of such harmonization, there has also been a drop in the level of public suspicion of seeming attempts to standardize products throughout the Community in earlier years.

The second main instrument, the so-called 'new approach' to achieving harmonization of key minimum standards for goods, has been in operation since 1985 and has substantially accelerated work in this area. The first Directive under the new approach, covering standards for pressure vessels, was adopted by ministers in 1987, and the second, on the safety of toys, in June 1988. Others, including radio interference and various types of engineering, construction and medical equipment, are pending. The key to the new approach is agreement on the nature of minimum standards for health and safety, conformity with which would guarantee the right of goods to be sold throughout the single market. The detailed technical standards would be left to specialized bodies such as the European standardization organizations, CEN and Cenelec, to sort out.

These two bodies are at the heart of the Commission's third main policy instrument. They will play a key role in developing new standards in sectors where little work has been done under national norms, and especially in sectors where technology is progressing rapidly — in telecommunications and information technology, for example. The other main role seen for CEN and Cenelec is in the formulation of wider international standards, especially as the EFTA countries are members of the two bodies.

The fourth and last policy instrument available to the Commission concerns the mutual information Directive passed in 1983, which obliges the Member States to notify new regulations and standards. The Commission has the power to freeze the introduction of new regulations for up to a year, in areas where it considers EC-level measures are more appropriate. Of the 450

---

3   This was one of a series of influential European Court rulings which undermined the legal basis of many obstacles to free trade which had been justified by national States on cultural, environmental or other grounds.

notifications which have been made to the Commission since the Directive came into force, the power has been used only 30 times, which, the Commission says, 'implies a widespread acceptance of regulatory diversity, as long as this does not cause new barriers to trade'.

The next main category of technical barrier concerns the creation of a common market in services, which the Commission sees as one of the main preconditions for a return to economic prosperity. They are given equal prominence with removing barriers to goods in the White Paper, but they are also amongst the most sensitive of the proposals, given their economic importance to national governments. Progress in adopting the White Paper proposals in this area has been slow, but the Commission believes that the mutual recognition approach is the best way forward. In some service sectors, such as finance, a large degree of Community-wide legislation has already been brought into place, but needs to be completed in order to achieve a single market. In others, especially new areas such as satellite broadcasting, advertising, information and computer services, a completely new range of common rules will need to be developed.

In the financial sector, the Commission's approach up to now and, in general terms, for the future is to produce legislation which guarantees minimum standards in the areas of financial stability and prudential practice of financial institutions. To that set of basic rules, the White Paper puts forward a series of proposals which will further open the way for financial services to be freely available throughout the Community, mainly through mutually recognized licensing. A further set of proposals is intended to create a Community-wide market for investment, making finance available to business and industry from anywhere in the Community. The issue here is to provide free competition on the basis of minimum guarantees of protection, but the prospect of individuals or industry being free to seek finance and financial services from another Member State remains frightening for several governments. Just how far the idea of a single market for financial services can admit what the Commission calls 'a minimum of locally imposed conditions in some cases' remains to be seen. The hope is that a system under which 'home country control' is the basis of regulation of financial services will make it easier to accept the emergence of a single market.

Another key service sector is transport, where the Commission has come forward with proposals to deregulate every major mode. As we have seen, deregulation in the road-haulage sector now seems well on the way, but progress in other areas has been much slower. Only partial success has been achieved in the air-transport sector, where more deregulation has been hampered by national governments keen to retain full control of their major airlines, and of the system of agreements which have for so many years restricted services and competition on fares.

New service industries are growing up rapidly with the growth in technology, especially in information, data processing and other computer services. The Commission's general approach is to establish a coherent framework for the growth in these services to be encouraged and not hindered by a variety of national regulations. This is again a field where the establishment of common standards is a priority.

Proposals in the field of broadcasting are the Commission's response to the explosion in the number of satellite stations which are becoming available throughout the Community. By definition, purely national controls cannot possibly be applied to a service freely available to several Member States. Setting as an objective the creation of 'television without frontiers' the

Commission's strategy involves removing the technical and legal barriers to the free circulation of programmes. In this way it is hoped to enhance the Community's ability to provide its own broadcasting material in preference to programmes imported from the United States or Japan. The future is clear: satellite television will grow and probably prosper whether or not common rules and regulations are agreed by the EC governments and their partners in the rest of Europe. The strategy spelt out by the Commission would involve the coordination of national rules on advertising, sponsorship and child protection, in addition to Community-wide legislation on copyright and, controversially, a requirement to provide a minimum quota of material originating in Europe. Finally, the Commission proposed that a single technical standard for satellite broadcasting — the MAC-packet — should be adopted immediately as part of its recommendations for common norms for transmission and reception of broadcasts within Europe.

The group of technical barriers to trade also includes legal and administrative obstacles to the formation of enterprises operating across EC frontiers. Efforts to complete the battery of company law Directives will continue as part of the internal market plan, including proposals in the field of accounting, taxation and liquidation rules, and optional structures for Europe-wide incorporation setting out forms of board systems. And while the Commission has pursued its attempts to establish a Community-wide system for the prior notification and authorization of large-scale mergers, it has been forced to water down the scope of its proposals when faced with the opposition of national governments which believe the proposed system to be unwieldy. In the area of intellectual property — trade marks, patents and copyright — proposals have existed for many years to create a full Community framework, and in June 1988, the go-ahead was finally given to the creation of a Community Trade Mark and Office to replace separate national trade marks. The discussion paper on copyright, including controversial suggestions from elements within the industry that a levy should be put on blank video and audio tapes to protect authors' rights, were expected to result in formal proposals before the end of 1988, says the Commission, while the EC has already agreed to proposals in other fields, such as the legal protection of microchips for computers.

The final area of technical barriers more properly concerns people and capital, and one which the Commission is keen to stress. The single market, it makes clear, must be a benefit for people as well as business and to this end, the Commission's White Paper contains several proposals, some already adopted, on education, training, the free movement of professionally-qualified people and the free movement of capital. As far as individuals and their ability to work in another Member State are concerned, the approach again has been based on the principle of mutual recognition. In June 1988, an important step was taken with the adoption by the Council of Ministers of mutual recognition of diplomas and the rights for professional people such as accountants, lawyers, psychologists and others to set up and practise their profession in another Member State, with certain minimum requirements for the legal professions regarding an adequate knowledge of national law. This 'new approach' Directive in the social field replaced the sometimes painfully long approach employed before, which resulted in it taking 17 years to agree on the rights of establishment for architects and 16 years for pharmacists. 'By 1992', said one Commission official, ' a professional qualification will be as good as a passport'.

The complete liberalization of capital movements in the Community is an overall objective of the White Paper, including the freedom to transfer cash anywhere and to undertake financial operations in the Member State chosen by the individual. With the continued existence of controls on capital movements in some Member States, the Commission's statement that 'complete freedom of movement for capital also has implications for each Member State's balance of payments and increased possibilities for tax evasion' is something of an understatement. Progress has been made nevertheless, mainly as a result of the loophole allowed by the Commission for the possible reintroduction of controls on short-term capital movements in emergency monetary or exchange rate conditions. Final agreement by France, and possibly other countries, may yet, however, depend on some agreement on a system of harmonized withholding tax on bank deposits.

The removal of fiscal barriers to trade is perhaps the most sensitive of all, touching the core of national sovereignty over the levying of taxation in the Member States. The mere introduction of VAT in the new Member States as a result of their prospective or actual accession to the Community has been the cause of considerable disquiet and distrust amongst the public. Although the overall structure of VAT has been harmonized since the Sixth VAT Directive was adopted in 1977, these measures simply set down the method of assessment and the range of goods on which the tax should be applied. What it did not do was to establish the rates of tax, nor exclude the possibility of applying zero rates of VAT on certain essential goods and services. Left with the freedom to apply their chosen rates of indirect tax, the Community has ended up with a system where vastly different rates have been introduced by the 12 Member States, in many cases for the same products. As a result of these differences, various barriers, especially zero-rating of exports and taxation levying in importation at the frontiers, need to be maintained in order to adjust tax revenues due to the right Member State and to ensure that fraud or tax evasion are detected.

Excise duties have evolved in a similar manner, resulting in wildly different duties being applied, often for allegedly social/health reasons, on alcohol, cigarettes and petrol, and still no common structure for their application. An indirect consequence of these different excise rates has been the very lucrative and very popular duty-free shops on ferries and at airports throughout the Community.

A crucial factor in operating both the VAT and excise systems as they currently exist is that the correct allocation of revenue due to national exchequers is dependent on controls at the frontiers on goods passing from one Member State to another. Only relatively small savings can be achieved by transferring this task away from physical frontiers to administrations inland. And even then, this is not an effective alternative with regard to individuals, where the temptation to buy a range of goods in a low-tax country and consume or even sell them on at home, perhaps fraudulently, is considerable. The fear of a loss of business to traders in border areas, and potential tax revenue for exchequers, has resulted in a resistance to Commission proposals to increase travellers' allowances.

The Commission's proposals in the area of fiscal barriers are based on an absolute need to approximate rates of VAT, and to harmonize rates of excise duty on five products. The measures are believed to be the minimum necessary if the barriers to trade which currently exist are going to disappear in a single market.

The essence of the proposed new system is that taxation on goods and services sold on the national market would be the same as those sold in the rest of the single market, a principle already established in earlier VAT legislation. And to simplify the tax structure, the Commission initially proposed that just two rates — standard and reduced — should be applied throughout the Community to replace the three that some Member States currently apply. The lower rate, in a band between 4 and 9%, would be applied to essential goods and services, including food, energy products for heating and lighting, water supplies, pharmaceutical products, passenger transport and books, newspapers and periodicals. The standard rate would be applied, in a band from 14 to 20%, to all other taxable goods and services. The existing higher rate on luxury goods, which is as high as 38% in Italy, would be abolished altogether.

Broadly, the budgetary effect for national exchequers in most of the Member States is expected to be neutral, depending on the rate chosen from the two bands. But the Commission's services have calculated, after taking several other economic predictions such as price elasticity and effects of specific sectors into account, Member States would be affected in different ways: Belgium, Italy and the Netherlands would manage to keep the same level of indirect tax revenue, France would see a slight loss, while Federal Germany, Greece and the United Kingdom would see their revenue rise slightly. But the consequences would be much more marked for the remaining Member States, the experts suggest, with a considerable loss of revenue in Denmark and Ireland and a significant increase in Spain, Portugal and Luxembourg.

In addition, to forestall some of the opposition expected from Member States which continue to apply zero rates, the Commission acknowledged that the difficulties which some Member States could face might justify the granting of certain temporary derogations to avoid jeopardizing the fundamental objective of creating a single European market. The detailed objections which have so far emerged from certain national governments, notably the United Kingdom, are discussed in a later chapter.

The proposed changes in the system of taxation for VAT involve the principle, already incorporated into the Sixth VAT Directive, of taxing products in the country where the sale takes place — for all sales, VAT will be charged to the buyer at the rate applicable in the country of purchase, and if the buyer is the final consumer, the VAT will be paid in that country. If the buyer is subject to turnover tax, however, he will be able to deduct the VAT he has already paid in another Member State, and when the goods are re-sold, will have to charge the customer the VAT at the rate which applies in his own country.

A clearing system would also be introduced under the Commission proposals so that the Member State where the good is consumed received the VAT due to it from the exporting country where the tax is collected. The system has been described as a sort of central account through which the Member States would pay in or draw out, on the basis of information already collected from the returns put in by traders in each Member State. A big advantage to traders, says the Commission, is that they will no longer need trade within the Community as export or import business for tax purposes.

The solution to the wide differences in excise duties for the Commission is to propose single rates for five key products — pure alcohol, wine, beer, cigarettes and petrol — to be applied throughout the single market. For some Member States, the new rates proposed could have considerable consequences. In Denmark for example, where indirect taxation rates are relatively high excise duty on the five products would be reduced considerably.[4] The proposed levels for excise, says the Commission, were chosen as far as possible to take account of non-fiscal policies (such as health, energy or the environment), but it is made clear that a harmonized tax system should not stand in the way of a coordinated adjustment of such policies.

So far we have concentrated on the Commission's detailed proposals for abolishing the internal frontiers and other obstacles to a single market. These lie at the heart of the project to give a new impetus to European integration.

But they only form part of a wider agenda which also covers monetary, social, environmental and other policies. It is to this wider agenda for 1992 and beyond that we now turn.

---

[4] This is directly linked to fears that significant reductions of indirect taxes would exacerbate the problems of certain national governments in keeping budget deficits under control.

Chapter 4

The new agenda

As a direct consequence of 1992 a new European political agenda, or more accurately a series of different and to some degree competing agendas, is being created. Quite apart from the issues surrounding the completion of the internal market, these agendas also reach into social, monetary, environmental and other policies.

The Single European Act committed the Community to a great deal more than just the creation of a single market. Indeed the Commission has always believed that without accompanying policies — for instance those designed to achieve greater social cohesion or progress to economic and monetary union — there would be a real danger of the single market project itself failing.

Without measures to assist the economically weaker regions and communities, the restructuring of the economies of the EC countries — to say nothing of the adjustments which will be required by progressive monetary and economic union — could actually tear the Community apart. For that reason the Commission and most EC Governments accept that there has to be acceptance and willing cooperation in the process of change not just by the national decision-makers but by the mass of the population.

Work on detailed social legislation has, until recently, lagged behind the commercial and industrial preparations for the single market. However the new Social Affairs Commissioner, Ms Vasso Papandreou, has prepared a draft Charter of Basic Social Rights which is designed to address this problem and to contribute to the building of a citizens' Europe.

Ms Papandreou has made it clear, moreover, that she sees the Social Charter action programme as much more than a mere demonstration of social concern by the European Community or a means of alleviating the possible hardships created by future economic and industrial restructuring and development. A discussion document on the proposed charter prepared by Ms Papandreou stated: 'Given our social traditions, there cannot be sustained growth in the Community without social consensus.

In fact, the social dimension is a key component of the internal market itself and crucial to its development which must be consistent with an improvement and not a worsening of working and living conditions. Clearly the creation of a free market should not mean a lessening either of social protection or a deterioration of the environment'.

The planned Social Charter is intended to cover the following rights:

(i)   to work and to fair remuneration, as well as to placement services free of charge;

(ii)   to the improvement of living and working conditions;

(iii)   to social protection, particularly to those excluded from the labour market and including migrant workers;

(iv)   to education and training through life;

(v)   to freedom of association and negotiation (the right to trade union membership and to participate in free collective bargaining);

(vi)   to freedom of movement in the Community, equal treatment between Community workers, harmonization of conditions of residence and recognition of professional qualifications;

(vii)   to information, consultation and participation of workers in their enterprises;

(viii) to health, particularly in the field of prevention and health care;

(ix)   to protection of health and safety at work;

(x)   to protection of children and young people (notably a minimum working age and protection against physical and moral dangers), the elderly (including pension rights and minimum incomes) and the disabled;

(xi)   to consumer protection, including the right to information and to protection from environmental risks.

The initial approach by the Commission is to seek to remove all remaining obstacles to the freedom of circulation and employment and residence of workers in the Community. The labour requirements of the new 1992 market will involve the movement of all manner of workers, but specifically of specialist and qualified employees — including scientists, technologists and members of the so-called liberal professions.

The Commission plans to tackle obstacles to the right of workers to move and settle in Community countries other than their own, for instance, by extending the length of time for which a residence permit will be given for up to about 10 years. Another proposal would increase the period which a worker can spend outside the country of his residence without his residence permit lapsing.

The Commission will also want to coordinate the different national rules governing the social security rights and entitlements of migrant workers, to ensure they receive equal treatment to that given to nationals. And those workers, particularly in the public sector, who take early retirement should be able to transfer their pensions freely within the Community.

The removal of obstacles to cross-border investment, production and trade which will accompany the 1992 internal market will gradually, it is hoped, bring about a Community-wide labour market in the sense in which it does not exist today. The Commission believes for the present there is a need to establish minimum health and safety legislation affecting workers throughout the Community. As a result, there will have to be some harmonization of legislation affecting work and peoples' rights and conditions at work. The, as yet, unanswered question is at what level should these standards and these rights be set?

More ambitiously, the Commission would also like to encourage workers' rights and access to information, consultation and negotiation. The proposals build on an earlier draft Directive — involving very modest proposals on industrial democracy and workers participation in company decision-making which were advanced by two former EEC Commissioners for Social Affairs, Mr Henk Vredeling and Mr Ivor Richard. However opposition from centre-right governments and employers' organizations resulted in the Directive being shelved at that time. One new approach is to establish a new European company law statute which would afford companies certain privileges in establishing and operating in other EC countries not available to firms simply operating under existing national regulations. These could include the right to offset losses in one Community country against profits in another for tax purposes.

In return companies, which have to have minimum assets of ECU 100 000, which decide to freely opt for European status, would be obliged to implement some form of worker participation. The Commission proposes three different models of information, consultation and participation to choose from.

These include the West German *Mitbestimmung* model which would involve the election of workers' representatives onto the boards of their companies. Secondly there is a variant based on workers' councils which are commonly operated in Belgium, France, Italy and the Netherlands.

Thirdly, the Commission suggests a looser option in which workers and employers would negotiate arrangements providing for information and consultation. However, if it were not possible to reach agreement through collective bargaining the national authorities in the country concerned might be required to legislate for some agreed rights for European company statute workforces.

When the Commissioner for the Internal Market, Mr Martin Bangemann, unveiled these proposals in July 1989, he made it clear that they would be based on articles of the Treaty which allow for majority voting in the Council of Ministers. This was clearly designed to prevent them being vetoed by the UK Government which had expressed its opposition to any obligatory link between the statute, for which it also sees little justification, and provision for some industrial democracy.

In a developing international labour market where there are deep-seated forces making for industrial restructuring and technological change, there is a greater need than ever for effective measures to protect workers from the worst consequences of those changes. Consequently, the Commission is considering the setting of a standard form of employment contract which would guarantee all workers certain basic rights.

The European Trade Union Confederation, which groups all the major trade unions in the EC, insists such a development is vital. The ETUC has, on the whole, supported the internal market but it regards these proposals as essential forms of social protection without which workers will be vulnerable to increased exploitation. Without the right to greater information and consultation in industry 'working people will simply not understand, nor accept, all the structural changes that the internal market will produce, if they are only told about them when they are shown the door', was the way one leading European trade union official had put it.[1]

As part of the strategy to reinforce economic and social cohesion in the new single market, the Commission wants to mobilize the considerably increased structural Funds at its disposal as well as the specific programmes which already exist to help certain industries such as coal, steel and shipbuilding adapt to change.

Among the measures already in force in some of these sectors, which may be extended more generally throughout industry in the Community, are help with retraining of workers made unemployed by restructuring, financial help with schemes to encourage early retirement and also encouragement for investment in new industries and services which could create new and alternative employment.

President Delors has already set out the goal of providing for every young adult the right to a job, or to training or to further education. Moreover, the Commission wants to establish the right to training throughout the working lifetime and points to the trends which suggest that workers will in future have to change jobs increasingly often in a working lifetime.[2]

More generally, the Commission wants to develop what it calls a dialogue between the social partners — the trade unions and the employers. The idea is that such a dialogue would cover issues such as work practices, working hours, social legislation and the wider macro-economic policies being developed to further economic growth and employment. The first such tripartite meeting between the Commission and representatives of employers and trade union organizations was held in Brussels in January 1989.

It is far from clear how effective this dialogue will be in actually influencing the pattern and direction of macro-economic strategy. This is something still retained almost exclusively in the hands of national Governments. Some of them have — in recent years — resolutely turned their backs on the idea of organized labour having any role in shaping economic policies. However, the support of the Commission for the dialogue approach does offer the trade unions a platform from which to develop their ideas on policy for growth, full employment and social reform.

Much of this is welcome to the trade unions although they have serious reservations on questions such as whether employers will try to bypass them in consultation exercises with their workers. But the biggest concern of the trade union movement has been the danger that the internal market will lead to a decline in social standards of workers' rights, not to an improvement. There are fears of social dumping, by which is meant the temptation to employers to undercut existing social obligations to their workers, by moving or threatening to move to countries within the Community where social standards and safeguards are lower and the workers less protected.

---

[1]   Peter Coldrick, European Trade Union Confederation, writing in *European affairs*, September 1988.
[2]   Interview with Commission President Jacques Delors, *Libération,* 5 September 1988.

It would be an extravagant exaggeration to suggest that the kind of proposals for minimum Community-wide standards represent any very radical programme for social change at the European level. Indeed they have already been criticized for being too vague and for falling short of the measures needed to ensure that 1992 really does not worsen the position of workers in the most vulnerable industries, local communities and regions.

Even so, the case for a 'social Europe' is one which arouses little enthusiasm and has already triggered ill-disguised hostility among some Member State Governments. And EC employers' organizations have complained that such a social programme would increase production costs, increase the rigidity of the European labour market and risk making European Community companies less competitive on international markets.[3]

The UK Prime Minister, Mrs Margaret Thatcher, has also attacked the alleged tendency of the European Commission to indulge 'in social engineering'. And in a major speech to the College of Europe in Bruges in 1988, Mrs Thatcher bitterly criticized those who advocated the setting of new and improved social standards by saying this would risk the EC becoming 'entangled in a network of rules and rigid regulation which would stifle enterprise'.[4]

In June 1989, the UK Prime Minister went even further in an initial reaction to the debate on a prospective Social Charter. In an interview with the *Daily Mail* of London she described the ideas and values which formed the Social Charter as being inspired by the era of 'Marx and the class struggle'.

At the Madrid European Council in June 1989, Mrs Thatcher reiterated her opposition to much of the content of the Charter, notably provision for determining Community-wide minimum wages and maximum working hours. However, the other 11 Governments encouraged the Commission to prepare a declaration and draft action programme on social rights to be presented to the following Community summit meeting to be held in Strasbourg in December 1989, and in the meantime to press ahead with specific legislative proposals.

On the other hand, the trade union movement is far from being satisfied with the social strategy which has, thus far, been adopted by the Commission. And, it should be remembered, that most of those proposals have not yet even been discussed by the Council of Ministers. The trade unions are determined that the minimum standards for health and safety and conditions of work will not be set at a level so far below the best prevailing standards that they would con-stitute a threat to conditions negotiated by the unions in countries where workers have been able to secure major improvements in their conditions in recent decades. They also wish the agreed common standards to be legally enforceable.

Secondly, it is not yet clear what role is envisaged for the trade unions in the system of improved consultation and information at work. The ETUC believes that such consultation should be with the trade unions, as the established organizations of workers, but this is not necessarily the view of employers' organizations and indeed of Governments in a number of Member States.

---

3 *European report,* Brussels, September 1988.
4 *The Guardian,* 21 September 1988.

Although the UK Government is also opposed to any suggestion that the European company statute and the enhanced system of workers' rights which go with it should in any sense be made mandatory, UK trade unions are already angered that they might be excluded from any benefits enjoyed by their fellow trade unionists in other parts of the Community in the new single market. On the other hand the Federal German Chancellor, Mr Helmut Kohl, in a speech given in Brussels in October 1988, reiterated Germany's insistence that the Europe of 1992 had to be a 'Europe of citizens and workers'. The scene was thus being set in the summer of 1989 for a major intergovernmental debate on the scale and character of the Community 'social dimension'.

In all this talk about a single European market and European economic and monetary integration, it is easily forgotten that social standards differ widely from one country to another in the EC. Although comprehensive statistics are hard to come by, there is evidence to suggest that poverty is on the increase in the Community.[5]

It is true, moreover, that the gap between the richer and poorer regions within the Community is widening. A report by the European Commission[6] confirms that the accession of Portugal and Spain has contributed directly to a situation where the wealth gap between the areas of the highest and lowest unemployment was two and a half times greater in the late 1980s than it had been for a decade earlier.

The arrival of the two Iberian countries has had the effect of increasing the Community's population by 18%. But it also boosted the overall numbers of people without work by some 30%. Notwithstanding the undoubted economic boom which has been triggered in Portugal and Spain as a direct result of EC entry, Portugal's income per head is still about half that of the Community average while that of Spain is only a little better than 75%.

Part of the problem can be attributed to underlying demographic trends. There has been a markedly above-average growth in the labour force in the southern Member States of the EC. These countries have also found it more difficult to adjust to the decline of agriculture and traditional industries. While some have been successful in attracting new industry, much of this has been highly capital-intensive rather than labour-intensive.

Central to the case for the single European market is that it will create, more or less automatically, conditions under which the less-developed regions in the Community will be better able to attract new investment and jobs. This depends in part on the fact that wages — including 'social wages' — are typically lower in these regions than elsewhere in the Community. Moreover, working conditions — including working hours, holidays and fringe benefits — are frequently far less developed than in the older industrialized — and trade-unionized — areas of the economic heartland of the common market.

As we have seen elsewhere, however, lower wages and inferior working conditions are unlikely by themselves to be a sufficient bait to attract new investment and employment to the poorer

---

5 This was discussed at a conference on the theme of Women and Poverty in the European Community, held in Brussels, with the Commission, in November 1988.
6 *The Financial Times,* 21 May 1987.

regions. Modern companies will be attracted to establish in areas where there is an existing modern communications and transport infrastructure and where there is an ample supply of skilled and trained workers.

This is why the extension of the benefits of 1992 to the less well-off and developed regions — which are mainly, though not by any means exclusively, situated on the geographical periphery of the Community — will surely require massive social and infrastructural investments in both people and the communities in which they live. The question is whether the needs of these regions will — eventually — prove far greater than the resources available to the Community even with enlarged structural Funds which — the Brussels European Council of February 1988 agreed — are to be doubled in the period to 1992/93.

It is not just a question of the scale of financial resources. It is also a question of the rather narrow terms of reference which limit the purposes for which the infrastructural funds can be used. For instance the present regulations make it virtually impossible to be used to help provide decent housing for people of the poorer regions. However, studies in Ireland and elsewhere have shown investment in housing can often act as a trigger for refurbishment of a region and hence its attractiveness as a site for new industrial investment.

The national and regional differences in standards applies across the field of social policies. Nor is it just the case that the gap is a simple one between rich and poor countries or regions. It also divides the populations in the more developed north of the Community as studies into questions as diverse as pensions for the retired and leave and holiday entitlement have underlined.

One UK survey of pensions[7] carried out in 1987 showed that payments to the elderly of ECU 54 a week were strikingly lower than Italy (ECU 88), Denmark (ECU 90), the Netherlands (ECU 93), Belgium and Germany (ECU 120), although UK pensioners have to pay the third highest rate of contributions through social security payments of the 10 wealthier Community Member States.

There are also significant differences in the level of education, training, health and other social standards — even among the older industrialized EC countries and — *a fortiori* — between the richer and poorer Member States. It also applies to conditions at work where, in spite of Community-proposed Directives, for instance on maternity leave, there are marked differences in entitlement.

Virtually all EC countries do recognize the right to parental leave, including statutory paid leave for mothers with the right to return to their jobs afterwards. The Federal Germans do particularly well with parents having the right to take up to six months leave each after the birth of their child.

Italian mothers are relatively generously treated although paternal leave is very limited. In Belgium parental unpaid leave for between six and 12 months can be taken but if the job is then filled by an unemployed person, the parent can receive payment equivalent to unemployment pay.

---

7   *The Guardian,* 4 February 1987.

In the United Kingdom, only 50% of working women are entitled to maternity leave[8] because women are eligible only if they have been continuously employed for two years. However countries as different as the Netherlands and Spain merely require a woman to be employed and insured at the start of her pregnancy. There are also differences in a ratio of 4:1 in terms of family allowance benefits even among the richer northern EC countries.

The story is a similar one in the field of health — though in this area more than most statistics are to be treated with great caution. For example, Ireland spends the highest proportion of its national output on health care in the Community, and Greece the lowest of any of the European Community countries. However other figures show that life expectancy for men is shortest in Ireland and longest in Greece!

On the other hand, the figures for the number of doctors in the population are striking with France and the Federal Republic of Germany at about 25 per 10 000 of the population, the United Kingdom at 14 and the ratio even worse for the poorer Member States. Moreover, the systems for financing the health services vary enormously throughout the Community.

The very fact of the single European market and a greater future mobility of labour between different EC countries is bound to create pressure in the longer term for some closer alignment of these different systems. In the short run there is likely to be an increase in cross-border health care and a further growth in the already considerable private sector health market under which nationals travel to other countries for treatment which is more readily available than in their own Member States.

Already there has been a stepping up of collaboration between different European Community countries of research into health care — of which the EC programmes on AIDS and cancer research are prime examples. However, health care — like social security and other welfare related issues — still remains overwhelmingly a national competence and this will not change in the short run.

Much the same is true of education, although there has been a big expansion of Community and nationally-funded schemes for student exchanges — such as the highly successful EC Erasmus programme. In the academic year 1988/89 some 100 000 student months of exchange visits were financed by the Community, although the national governments had insisted on having the proposed budget for work in the field increased to ECU 85 million.[9]

Erasmus encourages lengthy exchanges to get maximum academic value and it is significant that, in spite of some lack of enthusiasm by some national governments, demand for places in the scheme far outweighs the Community's capacity to finance them. Meanwhile, slow but careful progress is being made towards mutual recognition of academic qualifications — in parallel with similar developments for professional qualifications. A Directive to this end was adopted during 1988 by the Council of Ministers.

---

8   *The Economist,* 22 August 1988
9   *The Financial Times,* 8 August 1988.

More ambitiously, there have been suggestions that there should be some harmonization of national educational syllabuses but this has met with some resistance by governments. Some experts believe the first breakthrough might be in devising an acceptable syllabus for European history to be taught in all EC schools and colleges alongside national history.

The Community has also attempted to take initiatives in the areas of education (through the Lingua programme proposals to encourage foreign language learning and teaching in secondary schools), in health (through the proposed coordination of health safety warnings on tobacco products), and provision for the elderly (through the proposal to extend to all Community senior citizens the concessionary fares and facilities available to pensioners in each Member State.)

These moves have not met with universal approval from Member States, a minority of whom believe policies such as the Lingua programme's impact on secondary schools should remain a matter for national governments (or regional authorities in the case of the Federal Republic of Germany). For the time being, most aspects of social and welfare policies will remain a matter for national rather than Community decision-making.

One could sum up the state of the European Community's 'social dimension' in the following manner. Formal proposals have been made in the area of minimum health and safety standards and for some elementary rights for workers to consultation and information. There are ongoing programmes to help the unemployed (mainly through training programmes) and to close the development gap between the richer and poorer communities, regions and national economies in the EC. But the scale of Community provision in these fields remains relatively marginal.

Looking further ahead, could this change? One reason for thinking so is the simple pressure arising from the increased mobility of labour and students throughout the Europe of the single market. This, it should be remembered, is likely to embrace the six Member States of the European Free Trade Association as well as the 12 EC countries, if the proclaimed goal of bringing about an 18-nation common 'European economic space' is actually achieved.

The spread of knowledge and awareness of how people live and work in different Member States is also becoming a fact of life. There is greater consciousness of the discrepancies in the standards of treatment in the sick, the elderly, the unemployed and other groups. This is likely to lead to even more demands — over a wider and wider area of social policy — that the best standards in the Community should apply to all.

Political parties inside the European Community are already beginning to debate the extent to which they should aim at common standards of social welfare in the future. As we have seen the European trade unions have a direct, immediate and very material interest in extending the better levels of social wage provision and working conditions to the less-advantaged regions — if only to prevent social dumping. Other social interest groups representing youth, women, the elderly, the disabled, the unemployed — among other constituencies — are also beginning to frame policy demands on a European scale.

Another factor which is likely to work in favour of a sharper social welfare focus is the Community's citizens' rights programme. This, for example, has already led to the Commission working on proposals to give all EC citizens the right to vote in the local election in the countries in which they live as well as the right to vote in European elections.

For all these reasons we are likely to hear much more about the establishment of European social standards in the 1990s, much as we already talk of European environment protection rather than purely national measures. But the debate is unlikely to take off unless and until the European political parties begin to specify what their views and vision of the Community are in future.

The single European market provides one framework within which it is possible to raise these issues. It may not have been the intention of those governments which signed the Single European Act and committed themselves to bring the single market into being. Indeed it was the very last thing some governments wanted.

Pressure for improved common standards of social provision is bound to meet with resistance from governments and other bodies who resent any further erosion of national State sovereignty by the European Community. It is also certain to be confronted by business and industry which will argue that increased social provision could cripple the development of industry by undermining the competitiveness of European firms on international markets.

Many of these issues surfaced during the campaign for the direct elections to the European Parliament in the summer of 1989. Indeed the European Parliament has already made it clear that it wants to have a bigger voice in shaping the European social dimension. For the time being this will be restricted to attempts by MEPs to amend the legislation which will be proposed by the Commission as a result of its Social Charter action programme.

But the newly elected European Parliament will also want to play a role in encouraging greater public awareness of common European problems and the need for common European solutions. Some parties have already drawn attention to the major differences in national social security provision and campaigns to raise minimum standards of social benefit for the poor, for women, for the elderly and for the disabled are already being promoted by special interest groups.

Of course the extent to which the Community moves further into this territory — as into economic and monetary union — may lay the basis for what President Delors has already said is likely to happen in the 1990s — the emergence of an embryo European Government. But this, however, is bound to bring into still sharper focus the delicate question of the balance of political power — of sovereignty — between the nation State and the European Community.

It may be that any breakthrough towards greater political union in the 1990s, if it occurs, will take place less as a result of pressure on the national governments from the Commission than as a result of the growing self-assertion of the European Parliament. There is growing realization among voters that there is a striking and increasing 'democratic deficit' in the Community. This can only grow as a result of the single market and the continued drift of day-to-day governance of the Community to Brussels — meaning primarily to the Council and its many intergovernmental offshoots as well as to the Commission.

The great difficulty with this process is that it inevitably centralizes power in a way which many people find unacceptable. The question is whether there are other tendencies, over and above the empowerment of the European Parliament, which can be encouraged to counter undue centralization.

One obvious solution would be for greater power to be devolved from the national State to regional and local government. Some Member States — such as the Federal Republic of Germany, Italy and Spain have highly developed systems of devolved government and the growing liaison between European Community institutions and regional administrations has been a striking feature of recent years.

The Delors Commission, and the Regional Affairs Commissioner, Mr Bruce Millan, in particular, have been keen to develop these contacts more generally with regional and local bodies throughout the Community. A standing conference of local authorities has been set up to advise and liaise with the Commission. Some national States are fearful that this might lead to Brussels bypassing national bureaucracies in the preparation and execution of regional development strategies in future years.

The question is one with immediate practical implications. For example, new rules governing the financing of EC structural Fund investment in the Member States tightens the regulations governing so-called 'additionality by national governments'.

In the past EC Governments tended to ignore Community rules which required them to match Community finance with new public spending of their own in the development of the chosen regional or social project. With the doubling of EC structural Funds, and the move to majority voting in the Council of Ministers, these regulations are being strengthened and Finance Ministers and Treasuries may no longer be able to pocket the EC money rather than commit additional funds of their own.

Partly to ensure this, EC regional authorities are seeking a closer direct link with the Community institutions in Brussels. The Federal German or *Länder* regional governments already have direct diplomatic representation in Brussels. How long before the other EC regions demand similar status?

Thinking further ahead, it might be possible to restructure the Community's decision-making institutions so that the primary authority for legislating in the Community passes to the European Parliament. The Council might then become a sort of second chamber or upper house in the new European Parliament. National governments would of course continue to play a major role in such a second chamber, but there might also be scope for representatives of both the regions in Member States as well as the kind of commercial, industrial, trade union and professional bodies which are currently represented in the advisory Economic and Social Committee of the EEC.

The scope of debate about the social dimension of the Community necessarily takes us up to and well beyond 1992. It will affect not just the way the single market develops but will also play a role in shaping public attitudes to the whole 1992 project. And it will inevitably touch on deeper issues of European economic and political union.

In the meantime, major political battles remain to be fought if even the Commission's minimalist proposals to give reality to the social dimension are to survive an inevitable mauling at the hands of national governments within the Council of Ministers. If politicians, trade unions and other interest groups with a commitment to and interest in the enactment of serious social legislation are not to be disappointed and disillusioned they had better not postpone any longer the task of mobilizing public opinion throughout the Community.

This chapter has concentrated on the wider agenda as it affects social policy. But of course this is not all of the story. Apart from monetary policy — dealt with separately — there is also an enhanced EC environment dimension.

Popular concern about the threat to the environment has been steadily increasing in the past decade — as is evidenced not least in the emergence of serious ecological or Green political parties in many Member States of the Community. Lead and carbon monoxide pollution, acid rain, the threat from nuclear waste, and the frightening despoilation of the Mediterranean and Baltic seas from over-fishing, effluents and the dumping of toxic wastes, are just some of the issues which alarm the increasingly environmentally-conscious Europeans.

Throughout the Community — and indeed Europe East and West — there is near universal recognition that action must be taken at national, European and, indeed, global levels. It is an area in which the Community has, in the past years, taken an increasingly active involvement.

The general approach of the Commission is to coordinate and raise the standards of environmental protection. But the whole area of ecological protection is a battle ground between society and industrial interests and lobbies — some of which do not disguise their concern that overly stringent curbs against waste, pollution and other environmental hazards may inhibit economic growth and industrial investment.[10]

We are going to hear a great deal more over the next few years about these issues. Will European consumers be willing to pay more, for example, for cars which do not poison the atmosphere through exhaust emission? Will an increasingly energy-hungry society be willing to move in more radical ways to energy conservation and the development of environmentally benign energy sources — such as wind or tide — rather than opt for continued reliance on nuclear energy?

Sooner or later economic growth itself or rather the priorities which growth is intended to satisfy is going to have to be redefined so as to be environmentally sensitive — just in the way that social cost/benefit analysis is now a legitimate tool in appraising specific investment or production projects. It is far from clear whether pressure for EC-wide tough environment controls will work for or against the transfer of responsibility for such issues from the national State to EC institutions.

On the one hand, action, for instance, to deal with acid rain or the protection of rivers which cross national frontiers, has to be conceived, executed and monitored on an international level. On the other hand, some EC Member States with relatively high environment protection

---

10 *The Wall Street Journal,* 14 October 1988.

legislation are understandably apprehensive lest the laying down of EC-wide regulations leads to a lowering of standards. So far little attention has been devoted to analysing environmental objectives in their wider social context — for instance as a stimulus for the development of benign technology and energy resources and as a springboard for sustainable growth and unemployment.

In all of this we may stand accused of going too far too fast beyond the short-run implications of the programme to realize the 1992 market. Can we safely assume that the Commission's own legislative programme will become a reality? It is now time to turn to the issue of whether and when it will all actually happen.

Chapter 5

Will it all happen?

Until now we have assumed that the Commission's proposals for the completion of the single market — as well as many of the accompanying monetary and social measures — will not only be implemented but also implemented within the timetable laid down by the Commission. Indeed this assumption is also at the heart of the analysis of the direct and indirect effects on the European economies on employment and living standards which was made in the Cecchini report to the Commission published in 1988.

But how realistic is it to assume that the full programme of proposals will be fully adopted by the Community's decision-making institutions (above all by the Council of Ministers)? And how realistic is it to conclude that the whole process will be completed by the end of 1992?[1]

The Commission appears confident that the full programme can and will be achieved within the decreed timetable. However, in an interview with the French newspaper *Le Figaro* on 21 October 1988, President Delors appeared to hint that there might have to be a delay — perhaps even to 1995 — in the resolution of some key but highly sensitive and politically controversial dossiers. Subsequently, Mr Delors said he was referring only to possible derogations — or permitted periods of delay allowed to Member States which have serious political problems in implementing aspects of the 1992 legislation. He insisted the legislative timetable itself must and would go ahead as planned. Matters may not be quite that simple.

We know enough about the political reactions of some Member States to key aspects of the 1992 proposals — including the complete physical removal of frontier controls and the approximation of existing national rates of value-added tax and excise duties — to know that these will be bitterly fought within the Council.

There are question marks over some other elements of the programme. These include aspects of the creation of a single financial services market, the reconciliation of widely different national technical and industrial standards, as well as the complete liberalization of capital movements throughout the entire Community.

---

[1] In November 1988, Lord Cockfield presented his interim report on the progress of internal market legislating indicating that, at the half-way point, the Community was broadly on track, with about 45% of the 279 legislative proposals agreed in principle. But he warned that the very slow progress over indirect taxation remained a source of concern.

There are, sooner or later, going to be other areas of doubt and potential political difficulty. What, for instance, will be the impact of the single market on the Community's very different regions and national economies? What will be the effect of the debate about social cohesion on the 1992 timetable? And what will be the repercussion on the internal market of the debate which has to get properly under way with the Community's international trading partners about its future policy on trade liberalization?

At present the 1992 project is subsumed in a sense of near euphoria. After years of stagnation the Community is seen to be moving forward once more. The advantages and gains from eliminating national and other barriers to a single market are — at this stage — understood more clearly than the possible negative impact of liberalization and integration on the vulnerable sectors of the European Community economies.

Those responsible for *Eurobarometer* — the regular Commission supported poll of public opinion in the Community — have warned that public reaction to 1992 in most Member States, though not the Federal Republic, is still going through an initial honeymoon phase.[2] Inevitably this will change, at least to some extent, when the pattern of potential commercial and economic winners and losers in the process of creating the single market becomes clearer.

One danger for the Commission's overall strategy is that the greater the dilution of its programme for the single market, the more the promised economic benefits may diminish. On the other hand the desire of most, if not all, Community Governments to maintain the sense of political momentum generated by the 1992 mission, remains the most credible reason for believing that the great bulk of the programme will become Community law within the original timetable envisaged.

That said, it is important to look in somewhat greater detail at the specific problem areas which are likely to arise before the end of 1992. They raise not merely difficult technical questions but also point up at least a potential conflict of political or economic interest involving both different EC Governments and a wide range of sometimes powerful economic, industrial, consumer and trade union interests.

The first and most immediate area of conflict is likely to be about the scale of any actual physical dismantling of national frontier controls within the Community. The UK Government has already served notice that it will oppose the removal of all national control over the movement of people across the Community's frontiers where it judges that this might weaken its effectiveness in the struggle against crime, notably drug smuggling and terrorism.

The UK police and customs authorities have already claimed that the abolition of frontier controls could lead to a big increase in cross-border drug smuggling.[3] Some anti-terrorist experts have drawn equally dire conclusions, warning — in the words of Professor Paul Wilkinson of Aberdeen University, that by premature abolition of national border controls 'you are virtually saying, if you have a gun and want to travel, then come to Europe'.[4]

---

2   See *Eurobarometer* published by the European Commission in July 1988.
3   *The Wall Street Journal,* 3 August 1988.
4   Op. cit.

Another expert, Dr Robert Kupperman, of Georgetown University, Washington, claims that tighter controls on the Community's external frontiers with the rest of the world would be less effective than maintenance of national controls. 'Terrorists will go to the softest points ... You cannot totally prevent terrorists but you can up the costs to them', says Dr Kupperman. 'Without border controls it is inevitable that there will be major terrorist incidents'.[5]

The UK Home Secretary, Mr Douglas Hurd, has also publicly voiced his concern that the UK's tight national controls in illegal immigration could be seriously undermined by the 1992 proposals. While his Prime Minister, Mrs Thatcher, has also cast doubt on the effectiveness of frontier controls on would-be immigrants from the Third World in some countries in the Community.[5]

She told one journalist that strong national frontier controls would have to be kept to prevent people from Third World countries 'getting in for a short stay, moving around Europe, taking up residence — we would not know anything about it — and making great demands on our social services'.[6]

UK sensitivities on such questions as control of rabies and the impact abolition of border controls might have on animal health go well beyond the usual preoccupations of politicians or national bureaucrats. They reflect the deepseated traditions of a people used to thinking of themselves as a protected island race. It is significant in this context that Ireland, as well as the United Kingdom, is deeply sceptical about the proposed abolition of frontier veterinary controls, partly because of their success in preventing the spread of rabies, by insisting on retaining strict national border controls.

The Commission and many other experts, however, believe the physical removal of national border controls is politically and psychologically vital if the whole 1992 mission is to have popular credibility. They naturally dispute the arguments of sceptical national authorities.

There are, moreover, experts who question the case for maintaining the existing border controls over the movement of peoples within the EC as being necessary for effective surveillance and control over crime and terrorism. They point to the increasing use of sophisticated technologies and techniques for tracking drug smuggling or terrorism independent of frontier controls, which are now available to the police and other State agencies in the European Community. In most Member States there are also strong bodies of civil libertarians who oppose national controls on cross-frontier movements.

Indeed there is a more general civil liberties concern that the switch of frontier controls from the Community's internal to its external borders will be used to exclude immigrants, migrant workers and political refugees from non-EC and, specifically, Third World countries. The coordination of State policies on these questions, which takes place in the so-called Trevi Committee of Community Justice and Interior Ministers is seen by organizations such as Cedri — the Com-

5   Op. cit.
6   *The Financial Times*, 7 July 1988.

mittee for the Rights of Immigrants and Political Refugees — as a means of institutionalizing racist and illiberal attitudes within the EC. Statistics published in 1988 do tend to confirm the impression that Community Member States have already become far less ready than hitherto to recognize appeals for refugee status.

There is also something inconsistent about the desire of some in the United Kingdom to retain passport control at its national frontiers in order to counter terrorism. After all, the biggest problem in this area, the UK authorities have always claimed, is terrorist activity across the Irish border where no passport control exists at all.

However the UK government is certainly not the only government for whom the abolition of border controls poses serious problems. France, for example, wished to retain a system of visa for all visitors from third countries, whatever the arrangements made in other Community Member States. But France has now lifted its restrictions for Council of Europe countries apart from Turkey.

The Danish Government is also concerned that, as a consequence of the abolition of controls between Community Member States, it might have to impose controls on the movement of peoples from other Scandinavian countries within the Nordic Union, of which Denmark is also a member. Denmark's EC partners say that otherwise Finns or Icelanders for example, would have the same automatic right of free movement throughout the Community as EC citizens — something to which other visitors from third countries would not be entitled.

In spite of these problems there is little doubt that the prospect of an end to time-consuming and often needless passport and other frontier controls is highly popular with the European Community travelling public. It follows that any significant retreat from this objective would diminish the appeal of the whole 1992 project to many people. Indeed the entire exercise might, as a consequence, come to be seen as of more relevance to businessmen and financiers than to the generality of European Community citizens.

It may be that the only compromise which will guarantee the removal of physical border controls would be one in which the United Kingdom (and perhaps Ireland) are given a derogation — as exemptions from EC Directives are known in EC jargon — to maintain their present border controls for a temporary period. But this would not be popular with UK travellers who have been promised faster and less troublesome access to 'the Continent' as a result of the opening of the Channel Tunnel link with France which is due to come into operation a few years after 1992. On the other hand, the UK authorities did take some steps in the summer of 1989 to speed the processing of European Community passport holders through its airports.

The second of the most immediately difficult issues seems certain to be taxation policy. At the heart of the proposals for 1992 put forward by Lord Cockfield, the single-minded Commissioner, who was in charge of the single market strategy until he was replaced by the UK Government at the end of 1988, is the approximation of national rates of VAT and excise duties.

The Commission's insistence on this element in its proposals arises from its conviction that without some narrowing of tax rates there would be a serious risk of trade being deflected across frontiers from States with relatively high taxation to States with relatively low rates. And that, the Commission fears, could jeopardize the whole strategy of opening the frontiers by providing a permanent temptation for national governments to re-impose some kind of controls on cross-border trade.

This philosophy was summed up by Lord Cockfield in an address to the Biscuit, Cake, Chocolate and Confectionery Alliance. 'No one can complete the internal market unless there is a substantial measure of approximation of indirect taxes', he said. 'No way can one abolish the internal frontiers which is one of the major objectives laid down in the Single European Act, unless there is a substantial measure of approximation of indirect taxation. That is the lesson of 30 years of experience and intensive study which over the period has produced no other solution![7]

Neither the Commission nor anyone else — it should be stressed — is currently suggesting complete harmonization of indirect tax rates. As we have noted earlier the Commission wants to do three things:

First, to change the way and time in which VAT is collected so that a supplier of an input to the production process will pay VAT at the local rate, the company buying the supply would pay the difference between the amount of VAT paid by the supplier and that due on the sale of the good or service. Because national governments would necessarily receive VAT payments on the entire amount of consumption in their country — where the good or service was exported — the Commission has suggested a clearing house be established within the Community to refund governments who have received less VAT revenue than their due.

Secondly, the Commission wants all national VAT rates, which range from zero to 38%, to be simplified into two bands: one of 4% to 9% and another of 14% to 20%, covering identical goods in each band. Thirdly, there would be a harmonization of customs duties on alcoholic drinks, tobacco products and mineral oils and a change in the system of administration.

There are certain to be a number of very serious political objections to this plan. The UK and Irish Governments are firmly opposed to having to end the arrangements under which a number of essential goods, notably food, are zero-rated for VAT purposes.

The Danish and Irish Governments, which rely heavily on indirect taxes — 35% of GDP and 44% of GDP, respectively — to finance their very large government deficits would face a serious loss of revenue if VAT rates had to be reduced. Conversely, a number of countries — notably Luxembourg currently charge a VAT rate of only 12% and fear a threat to some key industries — such as financial services, if they had to raise VAT rates.

Spain is concerned with the social and inflationary effects of having to raise its national VAT rates as sharply as implied in the Commission proposals. France meanwhile has already expressed worry that the abolition of border controls might lead to French people crossing the border to buy cars in the Federal Republic of Germany — where there is a lower VAT rate. The same could happen between the Federal Republic of Germany and Denmark.

These are just some of the seemingly intractable problems which have emerged from the first attempts by European Community Finance Ministers in reacting to the Commission's VAT

---

7   *The Times,* 6 June 1988.

strategy. Unlike the question of physical border controls, a majority of the 12 EC Governments have some complaint with the proposed approximation of indirect taxes, although only the United Kingdom — and probably Luxembourg — appear to be opposed to the principle of approximation.

It should also be pointed out that the experts are by no means united in the view that substantial approximation is vital if the single internal market is to survive. To the contrary some point to the experience of the United States which has a very successful internal market but where VAT rates between individual states vary significantly, without producing a serious problem of trade deflection.

It was Lord Cockfield's determination to defend his VAT proposals in the face of criticism from UK Ministers which seems to have led the UK Prime Minister, Mrs Thatcher, not to reappoint him as the United Kingdom's senior Member of the new Commission which took office in January 1989. Without Lord Cockfield, and given the mounting chorus of opposition to its plans, it seems almost certain that the new Commission will come under pressure to retreat — or at least delay — on the implementation of key aspects of its VAT proposals. Indeed, during 1989 the new Commissioner for Fiscal Policy, Mrs Christiane Scrivener, signalled her willingness to adopt a more flexible stance.

One possibility is that proposals are adopted by the Council but that individual countries with serious problems in agreeing to approximation may be given derogations, at least until the end of 1992, to gradually fall into line. But this is unlikely to be accepted in the case of the UK where the Labour Opposition will try to ensure that Mrs Thatcher's pledge not to tax food or children's clothing is honoured to the last detail.

It might be possible to meet the 'French problem' by narrowing the upper band of VAT rates for luxury goods — say from 16% to 18% — to deter cross-border trade distortion. But this would make the problem worse for countries such as Denmark, Ireland and Luxembourg.

It might also be possible to sanction the VAT approximation in some Member States but not all. This might appeal to some, but would risk the fracturing of the internal market — and by extension the European Community as such — into the kind of two-tier or two-speed Community which many are convinced would eventually undermine its political coherence.

A third possibility is that frontier controls will be abolished but VAT and excise duty rates are left intact. This might at the end of the day be the best available deal, even from the Commission's point of view. After all, the main point of the indirect tax approximation is to facilitate opening the borders and if this can be assured otherwise, that might be acceptable. But if, in practice, countries with higher VAT rates were threatened with a serious loss of trade to cross-border competition in lower VAT States, how long would it be before frontier controls were reimposed?

In the longer run, some experts predict, the United Kingdom and Ireland for their own reasons of fiscal policy, will eventually abandon the zero-rating principle. However, this seems unlikely without some radical system of compensation for the poorest sections of society which would be hardest hit by the taxation of essential goods such as food.

Meanwhile the proposed harmonization of excise duties poses equally difficult problems. In Denmark it would lead to a fall in the retail price of cigarettes of some 44%, 90% in the case of Portugal, which would lead to a significant loss of exchequer revenue and certainly be seen as moving in a perverse sense in terms of the public health debate on smoking and cancer.

On the other hand, there are forecasts that approximation of VAT rates could lead to a 170% increase in Greek cigarette prices. And there are almost equally likely to be movements in opposite ways in the price of petrol, spirits, wine and beer, as a result of the harmonization of excise duties. All of this is, inevitably, going to provide ready ammunition for hostile political lobbies in Member States.

Indirect taxation remains a difficult and sensitive issue, but by the autumn of 1989 the prospects for a compromise agreement had been signally improved as a result of new proposals by the Commission.

Mrs Scrivener, who succeeded Lord Cockfield in the taxation portfolio, scaled down the original plan to approximate indirect tax rates. In May 1989 she announced that the Commission was ready to propose a minimum VAT band of between zero and 9% — offering the prospect of the United Kingdom being able to keep zero rates for certain sensitive items such as food — and a higher rate starting at about 15% but without a ceiling.

On the issue of excise duties, the Commission accepted that the problems of agreeing a single rate were insuperable and may propose a series of tax bands or minimum rates for different items such as petrol, alcohol, cigarettes and perfume. Serious problems remain to be solved such as the precise mechanism for compensating countries for the VAT paid on exports with a system of border controls which would undermine the central purpose of scrapping internal frontiers in the developing Community internal market.

The most likely compromise may involve some kind of clearing house to regulate VAT transaction between Member States. However, industry is hoping that as much trade as possible will be removed from the clearing house system. On the other hand the prospective deal on excise duties will almost certainly spell the death knell of so-called duty-free and shopping for travellers within the European Community.

The sheer complexity of the Commission's single market strategy is likely to produce other potential conflict points when detailed proposals are eventually debated by the Council of Ministers. However, they are unlikely to be so immediate or substantial a problem as either ending the physical border controls or approximating indirect tax rates.

One area which is progressing more smoothly than Brussels had originally feared is the creation of a genuine single market for financial services. The goal of creating a common financial area which would ensure freedom to provide financial services throughout the Community ranging from banking and insurance to investment and corporate finance will necessarily involve an integrated European capital market. The planned liberalization of the movement of capital for stocks, shares and bonds for financial transfers and commercial credits throughout the entire Community is ambitious however, and only a minority of Member States have yet achieved full liberalization. However all have now agreed in principle to fall into line over the coming years.

Towards the end of 1988 a further, unexpected, problem emerged which cast some doubt on the willingness of France in particular to complete the promised full liberalization of capital movements. President Mitterrand told the European Council at Rhodes in December 1988, that the total abolition of foreign-exchange controls would only be possible if the Community agreed a harmonized system of withholding taxes on bank deposits. Without such tax, the authorities in Paris suggested, capital decontrol could lead to a massive destabilizing flight of capital to countries without a capital withholding tax. In spite of this the 12 are deeply divided about the very principle of what some describe as a tax on savings and others regard as an essential curb on disruptive speculative capital flows.

As the Commission's own progress report on the European monetary system and the liberalization of capital markets made clear, the individual items in this comprehensive programme are to a large degree mutually dependent on each other. 'Full capital liberalization and the smooth functioning of the European monetary system throughout the European Community are necessary but not sufficient conditions to attain the degree of financial integration necessary to create a common financial area', the report stated.

'This requires also the free provision of financial services, for which, the movement of capital is often only a support,' it went on. 'It requires that there can be no discriminatory treatment, that conditions of competition between suppliers of financial services should not be distorted by factors such as divergences in prudential regulations or excessive disparities in taxation'.[8]

Serveral problems suggest themselves in this approach. The first is that full capital liberalization may yet prove both politically and economically difficult for some of the southern European Member States. The risks involved for the Greek, Irish, Portuguese and Spanish economies are not negligible and we do not yet know what would be the impact on stronger economies, such as those of France and Italy, where some controls on capital movements remain in force. However, in June 1989 the Spanish Government announced it would complete planned capital liberalization and peg the peseta in the exchange-rate mechanism of the EMS by July 1990.

Then there is the related question of the smooth functioning of the EMS. It is difficult to disagree with the Commission's view that the system must be strengthened if there is to be full freedom of movement of capital within the Community. As a minimum this must surely involve the full participation in the exchange-rate mechanism of the EMS by those countries whose currencies still float freely outside the ERM, notably the UK. Indeed, the full realization of Community-wide freedom of capital movement, unless accompanied by a stronger EMS and much closer cooperation of national monetary policy, might be an invitation to a massive and politically destabilizing series of foreign-exchange crises.

But stability will also require a more even-handed system of central bank intervention if the system of fixed parities is to be defended without unacceptable economic risks. At present virtually all the responsibility for intervention and macro-economic adjustment fall on the country with the weak currency. This is already a source of contention between the French and Federal German Governments. It is a matter for debate whether reforms in this sense will take us faster

---

8 *Le Monde*, 19 May 1988.

down the road towards an EC central bank, monetary union and a single currency and if so over what period of time.

What is certain is that any steps in the direction of a more supranational EMS are going to arouse nervousness in some Member States. The UK Prime Minister remains hesitant about sterling being fixed in the ERM of the monetary system while the Federal German Government (and in particular the Bundesbank) remain highly suspicious about any changes in the operation of the EMS which might dilute the Federal Republic's anti-inflationary economic policies, or the operational autonomy of the Bundesbank itself.

It is not too difficult to foresee a scenario where all these issues get entangled together: no deal on capital liberalization without a stronger EMS including sterling, and no creation of a common market for financial services without comprehensive capital liberalization. It is going to take much delicate political footwork to avoid these issues log-jamming into a negotiating crisis. However, in the autumn of 1989, after the successful Madrid summit, there was renewed optimism about the prospects of greater monetary integration.

There are some secondary difficulties in achieving a common financial area, moreover. In most EC countries financial services such as banking and insurance are highly regulated, whereas in Britain and the Netherlands there is virtually complete deregulation. One result is that life insurance premiums are twice as cheap in the United Kingdom as anywhere else in the European Community.

This sometimes leads to a rather different tone of voice being adopted by the financial lobbies in the UK and some other EC countries. At one conference in Brussels the general manager of General Accident, the UK insurance firm, said, 'Although we respect rules, we do not want them to restrict competition'.

In the same debate however, the vice-president of the German Colonia insurance company, Dr Axel Biagosch, said that while they were 'quite unafraid of competition', German insurers 'did not want freedom without proper rules'. He added 'Our job is not to open up the market to foreign competitors, but to make sure we do our job as insurers properly.'[9]

Whereas some progress had been made by the end of 1988 on harmonizing non-life insurance and large risks insured against by businesses, progress on life insurance by individuals is proving very slow. Meanwhile, there are many obstacles in the way of regulations on investment bodies given the sharp philosophical gap between countries which practise comprehensive and detailed controls (such as the Federal Republic of Germany) and those (notably the United Kingdom) which run a self-regulating system of supervision.

The very different structure of the financial markets in the different Community Member States, and divergences of view on the character of both national and Community supervision and control, may further complicate progress in finalizing a free and integrated financial services market. Added to which is the, as yet, unresolved question of whether and to what extent, the Community should open its financial markets to third countries.

---

[9] *Eurotrends,* Brussels, May 1988.

The City of London, for example, operates a global open-door policy as far as the establishment of third country financial institutions is concerned. The UK has also opted for a system of financial self-regulation — rather than control by statute — for City financial institutions. As a consequence, the City does not like the proposed system of regulation of banking, investment and other financial services suggested by the Commission. Ironically, there are fears that the City might lose business to other centres which end up with less demanding regulations.

The UK was also worried at suggestions that the Community might only permit third country financial institutions to operate freely where an as yet unspecified degree of reciprocity has been negotiated between the EC and other countries. The United States Administration initially saw in this approach the germ of a potentially dangerous protectionism on the side of the European Community. However, the Commission made clear in the spring of 1989 that by reciprocity it merely sought to prevent European financial institutions being discriminated against in the US. At that point much of the transatlantic steam went out of the reciprocity issue. Other Member States are suspicious that self-regulation and the City's generally permissive attitude poses a potential threat to savers and consumers of financial services.

The whole question of the external trade regime which will operate under the single European market could prove another major obstacle on the road to 1992. This is in part because of the debate outside the EC, rather than inside, which has crudely been reduced to whether Europe will adopt a 'Fortress Europe' or a global liberalization philosophy to guide its external trade policies.

However in a communiqué to the Council of Ministers in October 1988, the Commission moved to allay fears that it was being tempted to travel down the protectionist road. The Commission underlined its commitment to the Uruguay Round of GATT negotiations to liberalize international trade in goods and services and insisted that an inward-looking Community would not be in the interests of the economies or the peoples of Europe. This message was strongly underlined at successive European Councils — summit meetings of EC Heads of State or Government — held in Hanover and Rhodes during 1988.

European Community Governments displayed growing irritation in 1989 with accusations that they were planning some kind of Fortress Europe. The retiring Commissioner for External Affairs told the United States Administration in no uncertain terms that 'as by far the largest trading bloc in the world the European Community has no interest in turning inwards or in adopting protectionist policies'. The clarifications about reciprocity and the strength of the EC's free trade commitments did go a considerable way to alleviating — if not removing — non-EC apprehensions about 'Fortress Europe'.

But the choice between 'Fortress Europe' and an open trading Europe is an oversimplification of a far more complicated range of options between outright protectionism and full, parallel and simultaneous liberalization of external trade with the Community's major partners. Some European industrialists do believe that this latter approach might result in key markets and control of key European industries being lost to the Americans or the Japanese. As a result the debate is already joined, for example, over what kind of curbs the Community should maintain over textile imports or shipments of Japanese cars to the European markets.

Industrialists such as Mr Jacques Calvet of Peugeot have warned that 1992 might develop into a Trojan horse for opening the doors to Japanese domination of European industrial markets. There is also some national opposition to the Commission's proposal that the five countries which currently operate national restrictions on Japanese imports surrender future regulation to Brussels.[10]

At present, Japanese imports of cars are controlled through voluntary restraint agreements with the United Kingdom — and (more restrictively) with France as well as through legal curbs in the case of Italy. It will be no easy matter to negotiate a Community-wide arrangement which does not increase the risk of Japanese import penetration in the markets of those countries whose governments have until now been solely responsible for negotiating voluntary export restraint agreements with Tokyo.

The whole question of imports is linked with the growing problem, as seen from the European Community, of dumping by exporters from Japan, and also newly industrializing countries of the Pacific Rim such as South Korea, Taiwan and Hong Kong. Indeed in recent years the EC has strengthened its already formidable armoury of measures against dumping. It has, for instance, imposed penalties on non-EC companies which, it judges, have attempted to evade Community anti-dumping duties, by establishing what have become known as screwdriver plants in Europe. By this is meant factories where locally produced component or design adds a small proportion of value-added to the end-product. One senior manager of the giant Dutch multinational, Philips, Mr Cornelis van Klugt, has warned European regional and local authorities against using subsidies to buy Japanese investment projects adding 'Japanese factories in Europe leave quite a lot to be desired in terms of employment, value-added and technology transfer ... They have often taken place in sectors where there is worldwide over-capacity and where European industry is struggling to restructure.[10]

In an attempt to address this problem in the case of the motor industry the European Community is proposing a minimum 60% local production element for such foreign established manufacturing car plants. However, industrialists in a number of EC countries, notably France, have suggested that this figure should be as high as 80%. The issue threatened to cause problems between France and the United Kingdom in the autumn of 1988 when a new Nissan plant in the UK began production and there were suggestions that the French authorities might restrict Nissan imports into France.

There is little doubt, however, that very many major European-based international companies are worried about anything smacking of a protectionist 'Fortress Europe'. European multinational companies typically have major production and sales interests in markets outside Europe. They could be hard hit in any tit for tat protectionist trade war between the EC and the other major industrialized trading powers.

The Commission is attempting to square this circle through an approach based on the reciprocity principle. This would offer access to the newly liberalized EC markets to third countries pro-

---

10 Conference organized by the Brussels Club, May 1988.

viding they reciprocate with equivalent access for European exporters. However, many questions remain to be asked about this reciprocity principle and it has already led to public criticisms from both the United States and Japanese Governments that it could disguise a drift to generalized protectionism in the European Community.[11]

The former European Commissioner charged with responsibility for External Trade Relations, Mr Willy de Clercq, has promised that it will not involve measures which could conflict with GATT rules. But there would be no unilateral concessions to third countries and that the Community would maintain some general import restraints — for instance over Japanese cars, textiles and some shipments from Eastern Europe — by sectors not covered by GATT rules.

In the autumn of 1989 the Community was preparing to unveil its strategy for the motor industry which would indeed scrap over a period of years the purely national import restrictions applied by France, Italy and other countries on Japanese car imports. However, there were disagreements about whether and for how long the Community itself should maintain any controls over such imports.

In spite of these developments, the US, Japan and others are not completely reassured. In the closing months of 1988 there were still mutual charges of protectionism being made by the major trading nations. Given the implicitly protectionist elements in some of the provisions in the new United States Trade Bill adopted by President Reagan, after much debate with Congress, in August 1988, some experts still feared a possible drift to a generalized transatlantic, or possibly a global, trade conflict in the 1990s.

These fears were initially heightened towards the end of 1988 following the failure of the GATT, Uruguay Round mid-term review conference held in Montreal. The breakdown in the trade liberalization negotiations was primarily due to a deepseated conflict between the EC and the US over the demand of the Reagan Administration for the complete abolition of all Community agricultural subsidies by the year 2000. Although the Twelve are committed to a sustained reduction in farm subsidies, and in particular recent levels of agricultural support prices, the EC fears complete withdrawal of subsidies would devastate the EC's already hard-pressed rural economies.

The eventual outcome of the GATT negotiations of agricultural trade liberalization will — more than any other single factor — determine whether or not the GATT round proves a success. Only if it is a success will there be confidence that there will not be a return to trade frictions and even open trade war between the major global trading blocs.

Other areas of potential problem with the Community's international trading partners include liberalization of public procurement and technical standardization. It is by no means clear that overseas suppliers will be given equal access to the Community's public procurement market nor indeed when European companies will have equivalent access to the public procurement markets in the US, Japan or other third countries.

---

11 Such objections were raised during September 1988 both by the United States Ambassador to the European Community, Mr Alfred Kingon and by a spokesman for the Keidanren, the Japanese Confederation of Industry at a conference on European/Japanese relations held in West Berlin.

To the extent that the European Community is — for instance in the field of television, telecommunications and information technology — attempting to get agreement of EC-wide technical standards, this could become a perceived agency for protectionism. If the Community fixed its own standards which are quite different from those decided on in Japan or the United States, then American and Japanese companies will face the additional costs of tooling up to produce for the EC market as well as for others.

Indeed in the case of high-definition television the Community and Japan have already decided on mutually incompatible systems. This is also likely to be the case over a wide area of telecommunications.

The unanswered, and for the present, unanswerable question is whether the Community's commitment to internal liberalization under the 1992 strategy is or is not going to be fully consistent with pledges to maintain a liberal world trading order and to the spirit as well as the letter of existing GATT rules. What is certain, however, is that there will be a serious political fight within the Council of Ministers over the subtle but significant differences of view about trade policy strategy in finalizing the external dimension of the single market.

Meanwhile, progress in agreeing mutual recognition of technical standards is also going to be a protracted process. Unlike the question of indirect policy, proposals to harmonize common technical standards raises — of their very nature — a highly specialized and complex array of issues.

Because of this the Community has already retreated from its original attempt to achieve — through regulation — total harmonization of technical and other standards. The sheer proliferation of differing technical standards and regulations affecting industrial products and processes created the spectre of a massive bureaucracy needed to determine and lay down all appropriate standards. This was something which — experts feared — could take to the end of the century to complete. However areas such as telecommunications are an exception where the Community will try to harmonize standards.

In its place the EC now stresses the importance of mutual recognition between Community Member States for technical testing and certification procedures. This would restrict positive EC harmonization to the determination of minimum standards for health and safety specifically where it affects the production and operation of equipment and machinery in industry.

This should speed up the process of agreement on standards in the array of specialist committees which have been set up to advise the Council. And decisions in the Council of Ministers relating to the removal of technical barriers — thanks to the Single European Act — can now be taken on the basis of majority voting rather than unanimously — as in the case of taxation.

Other problems cannot be excluded. Proposals dealing with the Commission's — enhanced — role in competition policy and its desire for a stronger role in controlling cross-border company takeovers and mergers in the era of a single European market were proving controversial and difficult to agree within the Council of Ministers.

There are finally three other, more general, factors which could delay the final completion of the internal market — particularly towards the end of the process in the early 1990s. These might be summed up as the regional factor, the social factor and public perceptions in the Community about who are likely to be the winners and who the losers as a result of the dismantling of barriers.

If 1992 exacerbates the economic gulf between the richer and poorer regions, communities and industrial sectors of the 12 EC countries' governments will come under pressure to take protective measures. In the nature of things one must expect from here on to hear more from those who stand to lose from the process of 1992 restructuring than from those who believe they will gain.

There is also the possibility of something of an economic self-fulfilling prophecy in all of this. To the extent that the Council of Ministers may have to abandon some key elements in its 1992 programme — such as indirect taxation — the more the macro-economic benefits claimed as a result of the supply-side improvements in the EC economies brought about by the abolition of frontier and other controls may be subject to renewed questioning and debate. Nor can there be complete confidence in the assumption made by the Commission and its advisors, for instance in the Cecchini report, that the cost savings and improvement in competitivity expected from the completion of the market will necessarily or automatically translate into more enlightened demand-management policies. Indeed the general European — and international — economic environment in which the 1992 market will be completed, is extremely difficult to forecast.

Clearly if the early 1990s are years of significant economic expansion and rising employment, this will encourage the liberalizing process — both within the Community and between the EC and its major trading partners. That, in turn, could be expected to encourage a more expansionary fiscal and demand-management policy from the Member States both individually and collectively. Expansion and single market liberalization would then form a 'virtuous' economic cycle.

On the other hand, the 1990s may be years of renewed economic recession, worsening economic imbalances within and between major Western economies. Such a background may be expected to encourage external EC trade protectionism and could make governments even more cautious both about the completion of the 1992 market and about the kind of expansionist macro-economic strategy recommended in the Cecchini report.

It was precisely because of the likely uneven impact of the removal of remaining national barriers and subsidies which led the Padoa-Schioppa report to stress the need for concrete measures to redress any imbalance in the interests of social cohesion.[12] And it was in this sense that the European Council of Brussels in February 1988 agreed to double structural Funds expenditure on regional and social development in the years to 1993.

The question is whether this will be enough. There are two points of view on this. The first, championed by free-market enthusiasts, is that at least some of the poorest regions in the Community stand to benefit most from the restructuring and the new investment which will be stimulated by the completion of the single market.

---

12 'Efficiency, stability and equity', published by the European Commission, Brussels, 1987.

Some pure free-market evangelists even believe that it could be the older industrial regions in the richer Member States — such as Germany or Belgium rather than the traditionally pre-industrial regions in the South which stand in the greatest risk from the new competitive forces unleashed by 1992. 'Euro-sclerosis' or the inadequate response of regions and industries to adapt to change, could indeed be a problem facing regions of the older industrialized countries. Indeed it could be that the Ruhr or Wallonia or the North of England will face bigger problems in the years up to and beyond 1992, than the potential 'green field' new industrial projects in southern Spain or Portugal.

This same school of thought cautions against an overly ambitious programme of social standards and welfare lest it undercut the capacity of the poorer regions to use their low wage cost advantages to attract industry and business. Investment, of course, takes account of far more factors than merely the level of direct — or even indirect — wage costs.

This is directly challenged by other economists. They are convinced that without a substantial and continuous transfer of economic resources from the rich to the poorer Member States — monetary integration and the possible single market itself — would become unviable. Indeed this was the message at the heart of the Padoa-Schioppa report.

The UK economist, Sir Donald MacDougal, who chaired a committee on European Monetary Union in the mid-1970s, has suggested a more radical approach. He believes that monetary union would require a level of European Community expenditure equal to between 5% and 7% of the gross product of the EC economies. And that was conditional on spending policies which were heavily biased towards policies to achieve geographical equalization of productivity and living standards.[13] To the extent that the Community moves towards greater economic and monetary union in 1992 and beyond, the need for far greater resources for redistribution to the more vulnerable regions will become acute.

The present level of Community expenditure, and the priority given to redistributive policies, falls very far short of this goal. Even the enlarged Community budget agreed at the Brussels Council in February 1988, will be less than 2% of Community GDP. While CAP reform and the planned doubling of the Community's structural Funds is a step in the direction of redistribution, it is self-evidently a far less substantial commitment to the poorest and economically most vulnerable regions than that urged as a minimum by Sir Donald and many other experts.

It is this argument which is going to be heard increasingly frequently from advocates of a European social dimension. Whatever the intellectual case for or against social spending, the extent to which a social Europe becomes a reality, rather than political window-dressing is bound to be a major factor helping to determine opinions in regions and communities who may perceive themselves to be at risk from the internal market. This in turn will surely colour political attitudes in the Member States to the whole 1992 process.

---

13 See 'The role of public finance in European integration', Brussels, 1977. The report was drawn up by a group of economists led by Sir Donald MacDougal.

It would not be unduly difficult, for example, for the poorer Member States to form a blocking minority in the Council of Ministers if the political perception gained ground that they would emerge among the losers in the 1992 process. This is one reason why, as we shall see shortly, the new social agenda, indirectly generated by the completion of the single market, is likely to become a focus of political debate in the Community in the early 1990s.

In all of this it would be wrong to lose sight of the sense of momentum and change which the very introduction of the single market has already generated in most European Community countries. Industry is already preparing to exploit the potential of the single market, not least by committing new investment.

In this sense there is a built-in dynamic in the internal market process which may well prove stronger than any doubts, fears or hesitations on the part of those communities, industries and regions which fear they may end up the losers. Writing in 1989 it is striking how the remarkable economic expansion in Spain appears linked to the desire of international companies to locate themselves in a favourable area within the new single market. However, this very process of economic expansion — involving as it does widening differences in wealth and economic opportunity — appeared during 1989 to be generating industrial and social unrest in Spain on a scale not seen for many years.

In any event, the political and social processes set in train by the abolition of all internal frontiers in the European Community will not be determined solely by short-term economic effects. Whether or not the full economic benefits of the single market anticipated by the Commission, industry and many others, proves accurate, subtle but important changes are likely to take place in the attitude of people in the Member States to the Community and what it stands for.

The very fact of the internal market will surely heighten the longer-term and wider debate about what kind of society Europeans wish to live in in the years up to and beyond 1992 and, indeed, beyond 2000. It is to the possible shape to be taken by European society beyond 1992 we now finally turn.

Chapter 6

Towards Europe 2000

1992 is as much a state of mind as it is a date or a precise timetable. There is nothing magic about 1992 as a date. The changes which the single market will bring about will take place over a period of years up to — and in many cases — beyond 1992. They certainly will not all materialize on the stroke of midnight on December 31 of that year.

On the other hand 1992 involves a process of economic, political and social change which is already well under way and which will not come to a halt when the existing European Community programme for the single internal market is realized. A wider agenda or rather a number of competing agendas for European union are slowly but surely being born and the outcome of the debate on these different European 'futures' will become a more and more important feature of politics in Europe to the end of the century.

One of the features of the birth process of this new Europe is precisely that there will be debate, competition and maybe even political conflict between the advocates of very different kinds of European future. This is not something to be feared or resisted. For the clash of differing political values, and competing social and economic goals is what will give democratic life to the processes of European decision making. As Jacques Delors put it when he addressed the 'Kangaroo' conference of European Parliamentarians in Paris in October 1988: 'Europe may be the last great adventure on offer to our people.'

What this means is that politics in the European Community Member States are going to become far less exclusively national in the future. Political parties will have to address themselves in far greater detail to the European Community political agenda than they have at any time since the founding of the EC.

Already, for the purposes of contesting European elections and advancing shared policies and goals within the European Parliament, the major political parties are increasingly aligned with their co-thinkers in transnational groupings. But more than this may be called for in the future. It may even be that the transnational groupings have to coordinate their national political platforms to the point where they form a single, basic policy matrix on which national variants are added.

That in turn could eventually lead to the formation of genuine transnational European political parties, as politicians from a number of different parts of the ideological spectrum have already tentatively suggested. After all by the mid-1990s, more than 80% of all economic and social legislation will be Community rather than national in origin. It may be that in these areas the economic and social policies of the party political 'families' have to have a primary European focus with the national element rather secondary — the exact reverse of the present situation.

Economic and monetary policy may prove to be one of the policy areas which poses the sharpest supra-national challenge in the run-up to 1992 and, to an even greater extent, thereafter. In the short run attention is likely to focus on the immediate measures which the central bankers and monetary experts believe should be taken to increase monetary cooperation and lay the basis for future monetary integration.

This is much more than a purely technical monetary or financial question. The European political parties are bound to pose more fundamental questions such as 'what are the basic priorities of progressive monetary union' and 'what system of democratic control and accountability should be put in place to ensure that decisions on EC monetary integration serve the broader economic goals laid down by the Community's democratic decision-making institutions?'

Other questions are raised such as what is the right balance between policies to counter inflation and those to maximize growth and employment. Moreover as the Community moves closer to a real economic union there is bound to be pressure for far greater common policies of public spending to encourage redistribution and prevent a narrowing of the wealth gap between the richer and less advantaged regions.

The debate on EMU is, therefore, likely to reraise the question about the right size for a European Community budget in the future. Moreover, if the Community is to be given far greater resources for investment and expenditure in the run-up to EMU, there is also bound to be a review of the existing restrictions on the spending policies of the Community.

On the other hand, without major steps to strengthen the present European Monetary System — and the fixed exchange rate regime which lies at its heart — some governments may prove reluctant to actually implement full capital movement liberalization. Quite apart from countries such as Greece, Portugal and Spain which are not yet members of the ERM — it could be that Italy and even France — will hold back unless they see a coherent monetary system capable of absorbing the foreign exchange market strains generated by sudden, unpredictable and potentially massive movements firmly in place.

In other words, whatever the doubts and scepticism of those opposed to a full central bank may be at this stage, the interplay between monetary policy and the 1992 programme of capital liberalization does point in the direction of such an institution. It may be that the Community opts, at first, for some interim arrangement such as the United States Federal Reserve was in its early days when it was answerable to its constituent banks and had very limited powers of its own. Although such a body would be a 'central bank of central banks' it would be a major step on the road to a genuinely supra-national central bank.

In any event there is a strong body of opinion among EC Governments in favour of strengthening the exchange-rate mechanism at the heart of the EMS. The participation by the United

Kingdom, Greece, Spain and Portugal in the ERM is seen as the *sine qua non* of even a modest strengthening of the EMS as a whole.

At the same time there is a desire to see the currency market intervention mechanisms within ERM strengthened in various ways, for instance by some reduction, in the case of Italy, in the permitted margin of fluctuation of the lira against the European currency unit. But hand in hand with this there may also have to be some change in the system of responsibility and authority for actual interventions by central banks, to assure the integrity of the fixed rate system.

This could mean at least a partial shifting of the burden of exchange-rate or even macro-economic adjustment from the weaker currencies to the stronger — notably the lynchpin currency in the present EMS, the German mark. Some modest moves in this direction were sanctioned by EC Finance Ministers at a meeting in Denmark in 1987, but — in the view of many — the present system remains unacceptably lop-sided.

Critics claim that the present system is still biased far too much in favour of the German mark and that the present rules of adjustment hide a bias pushing the European Monetary System towards deflationist rather than expansionist or growth-oriented economic policies. This is a highly controversial view, however and not one shared by all EC Governments — and certainly not all central bankers in the European Community. But it is likely to be heard with increasing force if the 1990s prove to be years of renewed recession and unemployment.

The powerful — and, it should be remembered, politically autonomous — Bundesbank insists that the economic success of the Federal Republic over many years is intimately linked to having a financial and monetary order which does not give an overriding priority to the maintenance of low-inflation policies. In its initial contribution to the debate about a possible European central bank the Federal German Government, in Bonn, and the Bundesbank, in Frankfurt, both stressed their determination that this should be the approach towards any Community-wide central bank.

These are areas of legitimate dispute. In other EC countries there may be a preference to trade a slightly higher risk of inflation if this enabled the Community as a whole to generate a higher real level of economic growth and employment. The 'growth' school in the debate about the future of the EMS will also point out that the German economy may in the future no longer so clearly be the best anchor for the Community's monetary and economic policies.

In the late 1980s some economists alleged that the German economy was beginning to show some symptoms of the kind of malaise which had long afflicted other West European economies. It appeared to be suffering from the internal structural rigidities in its economy which were making it difficult for German industry to adapt as readily and effectively as some others to changing international market circumstances. However, critics of recent trends in the Federal German economy were obliged to moderate their views when it became apparent during 1988 that the economic growth was expanding at a faster rate than had even been forecast by the Economics Ministry in Bonn.

For these and other reasons it will take a great deal to convince the more conservative Finance Ministers and central bankers that the centre of gravity of the EMS — currently based on the Federal German mark — does need changing. But there is a political problem raised with the question of just who should take the decision about EC monetary policy.

By and large the conservatives want the EMS — and *a fortiori* — any future European central bank — to be run by central bankers with the very minimum of interference from politicians. They will probably insist on this being guaranteed in the constitution of any such bank so that the central bank directors can, if they deem it appropriate, ignore the pressure from elected politicians whether on a national or the Community level.

Not everyone would be very happy with this kind of arrangement. In some countries it would be politically unacceptable on democratic grounds to give an EC central bank the degree of political autonomy enjoyed by the Bundesbank. It would be seen as legitimating economic rule by a caste of unelected and unaccountable central bankers rather than by elected politicians.

The argument goes deeper than this. The question of democratic control and the kind of monetary policy the Community might pursue through its own central bank are intimately linked. Some politicians see the role of a central bank as essentially little more than 'holding the ring'. That is it should be restricted to acting to counter inflation and ensuring monetary stability — while the key decisions affecting growth, employment and living standards are essentially taken by free market forces. On the left, however, there are economists who believe an EC central bank should be used as a positive instrument of public policy to achieve aims which included the optimization of growth.

The whole question of monetary integration is, of course, part and parcel of the debate about a single European currency. Again there is plenty of scope for disagreement about whether or to what degree a commitment to introduce a single currency is a necessary corollary of a deliberate strategy to pursue monetary integration.

There are powerful arguments in favour of a single currency however. The European currency unit — the embryo EC money — is in increasing use, albeit at present mainly as an accounting unit between EC institutions and some large financial bodies as a vehicle for a modest proportion of private and public sector investment.

However, the introduction by the UK Government of ecu-denominated Treasury Bills in July 1988, has led some financial experts to predict that the ecu could become 'a' — if not 'the' main denominator of investments and savings in the European Community over the next decade. Even so, others insist, there is no necessity to make the ecu a currency in the full sense of the word, especially if all the currencies of the EC are to be tied more closely to each other in future inside the exchange-rate mechanism of the European Monetary System.

The ecu could be introduced alongside and not in place of national currencies. There are precedents for this in the free circulation in Luxembourg of Belgian currency and of UK sterling in Ireland. But when it comes to such matters, sentiment and the psychology of national symbolism is certain to play a role as well as rational calculations about monetary effectiveness.

But in a sense these debates are secondary and largely technical. The real issue is whether the European Community national Governments will be willing — by whatever means and following whatever path — to move towards far greater, *de facto,* monetary integration. Two major factors will be working in this direction. The first, as we have already pointed out, is the internal market itself. To the extent that its smooth operation and its transparence as a fair system of competition requires a strong and common monetary framework, integration is likely to follow.

Insistence by the United Kingdom, for example, that it should continue to be free to allow sterling to fluctuate freely against those EMS currencies which are locked to each other within the ERM could, in the not too distant future, cause serious problems for the completion of the internal market. It would be idle to predict just how such a crisis would emerge, let alone, how it would be resolved. Even in the United Kingdom, which has hitherto insisted on remaining outside the ERM, support is growing among industrialists, opinion formers and even politicians for full EMS membership. A confrontation which put at risk the advantages a single market offers to UK interests such as the financial services sector, might lead to overwhelming pressure on the UK Government to fix sterling within the ERM proving too great to resist. This is all the more plausible since Mrs Thatcher's cabinet is already openly divided on the issue of sterling's full participation in the ERM.

It must be admitted that the sceptics and opponents of a stronger EMS do have a point when they speak of full EMS membership as the 'thin end of a wedge' which will gradually lead to a lessening of untramelled national sovereignty over other cases of economic policy. The question might be rather put: 'How effective can purely national monetary and economic policies be expected to prove in a period when — EMS or no EMS — the globalization of capital movement is such a powerful force?' Monetary integration — with or without a single currency — does imply recognition of the need for policy coordination and even decision-making at an EC level about key economic variants such as monetary growth and interest rates, as well as, of course, exchange rates.

But this in turn raises questions about the future management of even more sensitive areas of national policy making, including taxation and public spending. No one would deny that — for the foreseeable future — Member States will continue to play a major role in determining their own fiscal and demand-management policies. But the pressures on national Finance Ministries to avoid being significantly out of step with the rest of the Community in these areas is certain to grow even stronger.

The more interventionist-minded economic strategists see the monetary policy of a European central bank as being designed, where appropriate, to modify free market forces rather than act merely to reinforce them. As a result, the discussion over the role and character of an EC central bank is inseparable from the debate about the future direction of economic strategy.

However this is to suggest that the debate will take place between two neatly labelled factions: the monetarist anti-inflationists and the neo-Keynesian supporters of economic intervention. To start with, these divisions have in recent years become very blurred; most Keynesians now see a stronger role for monetary policy while many so-called monetarists take a far more pragmatic view of traditional doctrine about the relationships of money supply to inflation and growth.

On the other hand, there seem certain to be economic problems in the 1990s which raise different kinds of issues. For example if there is a period of marked slowdown of world economic growth over the next few years, to what extent could or should the European Community attempt to switch from an export to an internal consumption-led strategy for growth and employment?

In the 1980s the overwhelming consensus among European economists and business people was that the best assurance of European economic prosperity would be provided by the maximum openness to the world economy and, consequently resistance to all forms of protectionism. But will the choice necessarily be so clear in the 1990s if global economic imbalances are only to be reduced through a period of recession or worse?

It would be foolish to shut one's eyes to the prospect that the 1990s could see global trade conflict on a scale not seen since before the Second World War. Much will depend on the outcome of the global negotiations on freer world trade within the Uruguay Round of the General Agreement on Tariffs and Trade (GATT).

As the 1980s drew to a close the auguries were not so cheerful. The European Community was worried about protectionist trends within the United States, following the passing by Congress of a new Trade Bill in the closing months of the Reagan Administration.[1] There were also continuing frictions with Japan, and some of the newly industrialized economies, about the scale of their trade surpluses with the EC and continued difficulties of access to their domestic markets for European exporters.

The EC for its part faced considerable difficulties in reassuring its world trading partners that the 1992 market would not evolve into a protectionist 'Fortress Europe' as far as its external trade policies were concerned. But it is agriculture, and the US demand for the abolition of all subsidies and other public support for Europe's farmers which may prove the most tangible threat to a GATT trade agreement.

The Community has for some years recognized the need for major structural reforms in its common agricultural policy. A start has been made to switch financial support from price support and production to support of farmers' incomes. There is also recognition of the need to counter the explosive growth in agricultural productivity — sometimes at the expense of the environment — with a more balanced strategy for developing the rural economy.

On the other hand, the Community was able to report striking reductions in its agricultural surpluses within a year of the 1988 farm policy reforms. Reserve stocks of key dairy and meat products — the so-called food mountains and milk and wine lakes — fell dramatically — even to the point where there were reports of local shortages.

---

1 The European Community fears that the US Trade Bill could be used as an instrument of overt protectionism, particularly because of clauses which authorize such action where the US authorities complain of unfair lack of access to foreign export markets.

At the same time, thanks to the otherwise disastrous droughts and poor grain harvests in the United States and elsewhere, the gap between higher Community and lower world commodity prices resulted in a very sharp reduction in EC spending on export subsidies.

It is far too soon to say whether chronic systemic over-production is a thing of the past. Certainly the Community agricultural structural reforms — including schemes to take land out of production, to switch to organic farming and to penalize excess production — certainly are having an impact.

The encouragement of organic farming and the rejection of agricultural production based on excessive use of industrial techniques also reflects the dramatic impact of the Green movement in European society. Concern for the threat to the European and indeed the global ecology was one of the most potent political forces in the late 1980s.

Political parties across the ideological spectrum now accept that far-reaching measures must be taken to defend the environment and that all other economic and industrial policies should be scrutinized for the ecological impact. But the Green movement is also raising more radical issues which go to the heart of many fixed assumptions about the way a modern capitalist economy operates.

For example, how should we measure growth so as to take into account the sometimes damaging impact it can have on the ecological or social environment? Society lacks a comprehensive measure of the social and ecological costs of uncontrolled economic growth. On the other hand, it might be that Europe, with its rich cultural and diverse social history, will be the first to identify new forms of investment and production to meet social and environmental needs which are either ignored or marginalized within the conventional ambit of the market.

On the right these developments will be a challenge to advocates of a pure free-market logic. For example, it may be that the crisis facing our cities and major urban connurbations is only to be solved by switching our economic priorities away from mass production of private cars, for example, to new, more user-friendly forms of public transport. The question then will be, will the market-place be the best way of taking these decisions or should there be a role for democratic decisions about the allocation of public sector resources at a Community level to tackle such problems.

The debate about the kind of Europe up to and after 1992, is bound to touch on a wide range of other economic and political options. This is one reason why the debate on economic strategy will not fit easily into a traditional 'Keynesian versus monetarist' framework.

The case for the private, free market is well established and is supported by some powerful industrial and political forces. In this perspective, the European Community institutions have a very limited legitimate role, directly or indirectly, in economic and industrial decisions about investment and production. The dominant consensus throughout the European Community at present is that these decisions are best left to private industry.

On the other hand, the parties of the left are already beginning to think through their ideas about the role of transnational forms of planning and public ownership in the single European market of the 1990s.

For example, some believe it might be possible for the left to devise new forms of cross-border social ownership under which the Community might take a stake in major multinational companies? Some are attracted by the model of a European enterprise board under which the EC taxpayer could become part or even outright owner of the major multinational firms whose decisions have such a profound effect on the lives of workers and consumers.

There is also the related question of whether the provision by the European Community of public-sector funding for private capital should be conditional on securing a direct return to the public itself.[2] Even today the European Community makes available to private companies literally billions of ecus in grant aid, for research and development, partly because of the short-comings and the narrow horizons of the private venture capital bodies who are often reluctant to back long-term technological investment and new product innovation. But where such ventures prove successful and yield to private owners a handsome profit why should not some return — perhaps in the form of a right to convert EC grant aid into an equity stake — be made available? That said, it is certain that the parties of the centre and right will contend that such radical innovations are counter to both the letter and the spirit of the Treaty of Rome. Which is why it is possible that the 1990s may also see discussion about whether the Rome Treaty is out of date and in need of reform if not replacement.

Policy on competition as well as mergers, takeovers and monopolies is already very much in the competence of the European Community. Research and development is also a rapidly expanding Community area of decision making which, as we have seen, raises other and wider issues of public planning and social ownership such as what relationship should exist in future between the free market and wider public interests.

The balance between the national and the Community in economic decision making has already shifted significantly towards the Community. This fact has not yet been anything like fully absorbed by national politicians or voters. However it is interesting that opinion polls consistently report very strong voter support for the idea of a European Government, directly affecting economic policy making. This is true even in countries whose enthusiasm for the existing European Community is more muted than others.[3]

It would be wrong, however, to see the future as consisting of an uninterrupted line of development involving the transfer of more and more sovereignty and decision making upwards from the national State to the EC institutions. Paradoxically, the single European market and the wider array of measures to encourage European integration which apparently accompany it, may also indirectly generate a renewed emphasis on decision making at a lower level than the national State itself.

---

[2] For further discussion on this and related ideas see the author's *Trading places — the future of the European Community,* Radius Hutchinson/Granada Television, London, April 1988.

[3] See the *Eurobarometer* findings on this question published by the European Commission in July 1988.

The growth in the Community's so-called structural Funds directly reflects the political priority being given to balancing the internal market with more vigorous action to reduce the wealth and economic development gap between the richer and poorer regions and communities in Europe. But this could open the way to demands that a far stronger role be given to regional and even local government bodies in assisting EC institutions determine the most effective policies to help their own development.

Attitudes to regional decentralization and closer links between the regions and the Community, on the side of the national State, are ambiguous. In some countries, notably the Federal Republic of Germany, political power is already divided between the Federal Government in Bonn and the *Länder,* or regional governments while in others the authority of the national State in determining regional policies is almost total. In other Member States power is still heavily centralized.

It is not difficult to see a future in which regional bodies deal directly with Brussels rather than — as at present in most countries — exclusively through their national governments. The case for this is partly economic. At present some national governments can effectively save on regional development expenditure by transferring the responsibility for funding for some projects which they would otherwise have to undertake, to the EC, and 'pocket' the saving to the benefit of the national government budget and its funding requirement.

But this issue is also political and social. The most potent objection to the entire process of European union — including many of the accompanying measures to the single European market — is that it will lead to rule by a remote bureaucracy which is intensitive if not simply ignorant of the needs and aspirations of local communities.[4] This is yet another area of development which poses the basic question about the democratic legitimacy of the present Community decision-making institutions.

At the same time the 1990s will almost certainly see a further enlargement of the European Community. Already the 12 Member States of the EC and the six member States of EFTA — the European Free Trade Association — are negotiating the bringing into being of an 18-nation free-trade common European economic space.

It is far from obvious at the time of writing that the outcome will be satisfactory to all EFTA member States. Already in some — notably Austria and Norway, but also to a degree in Sweden and Switzerland — a debate is underway about possible membership. Indeed the Austrian Government submitted its formal application for Community membership in July 1989. The insistence of the Austrian Government that its neutrality would be permanent raised some objections that this was inconsistent with a readiness to proceed eventually to full European union. Others insisted that neutrality is in no way prohibited by the Treaty of Rome or the Single European Act.

---

4   Ironically this was a point made by the UK Prime Minister Mrs Margaret Thatcher, in her speech attacking European Union, at Bruges in September 1988. However Mrs Thatcher was less concerned about the demands of particular regions within the Community than the threat she perceived to national sovereignty in moves to increase decision-making at the EC level.

The political implications will be dealt with a little later. But, given the fact that countries such as Cyprus and Malta, as well as Turkey, are also interested in joining the EC, it is not out of the question that, by the mid to late-1990s, the European Community might consist of anything between 15 and 20 or more Member States.

And that is to leave on one side the evident desire of at least some of the East European member States of Comecon, the Eastern bloc trading organization, to have far closer economic, commercial and political links with the Community. Could it be that, towards the end of the 1990s, Hungary, Poland and possibly other Comecon countries will also apply for full membership? The Soviet Union, Poland, Hungary and Yugoslavia have already been accorded special guest status by the Council of Europe.

If enlargement on anything like this scale were to happen, the result would be to make the enlarged European Community a far more self-sufficient economic unit. This is not to suggest that an enlarged European Community would have any interest in running down its economic ties with the outside world. But such a Europe would enjoy a changed relationship with the world economy. For example an enlarged European Community would leave more leeway and potential for following its own economic policy priorities, without risking major negative effects on its external trade balance and so being vulnerable to the sanctions of disapproving international currency markets.

As we have seen earlier, the 1992 agenda does have important implications for social policy in the Community. The Delors package is now part and parcel of a strategy to see that the single European market strengthens, and does not weaken, the cohesion of Europe's very different regions, communities and national economies.

But how will these goals be translated into specific, concrete and credible social policy legislation? For the immediate future, the EC Council of Ministers is likely to focus on proposals to create minimum health and safety provisions, to push for corporate structures which offer workers a bigger say at work, to endorse enhanced programmes for training and education and to give encouragement for equal opportunities policies, particularly those designed to help women, ethnic minorities, the disabled and migrant workers.

In the second half of 1988, the European Community Presidency was in the hands of a Greek Government which outlined to the European Parliament in June of that year, its determination to give a higher priority to social policy. The Greeks were followed by the Spanish and French Governments in 1989 and the Irish Government in the first half of 1990, all of which have a political interest in seeing that the social policy dimension of the Community is given real substance.

Of course social policy, is, even more than economic strategy, highly politically charged. One well-known European Community Prime Minister has already expressed her distaste for what she described as a temptation for some in the Community to engage in social engineering.[5]

---

5   Mrs Thatcher in a BBC interview in July 1988.

But others recognize the need to restore a greater sense of partnership with the trade unions in restructuring the European economy for the 1990s.[6]

At this point a sharp distinction should be drawn between at least two different visions of a European social dimension. One is the kind of modest social safety net for workers in the single European market which most Member States are likely to eventually recognize is necessary and indeed a modest price to secure the cooperation of the trade unions in the economic and industrial changes which 1992 will unleash.

There is an alternative view of social policy. This starts from the recognition that there are unacceptably large differences in the social rights and entitlements of people in different parts of the European Community and the future single market and it should be a goal of future European Community policy that these are drastically reduced.

Social standards and provision of social services do vary enormously in the European Community at present. Health provision, unemployment pay, and other social security benefits, for example, in countries such as Greece, Portugal and Spain are a fraction of what they are in Denmark, the Netherlands or Germany. But can a single market, where all other special arrangements in national markets have been removed, be expected to operate successfully in the long term when the social wage varies to such a degree?

Of course the fact that they are relatively low-wage countries, in which social provision is often so rudimentary, is one, sometimes crucial, selling point for the poorer EC countries in attracting investment from firms wishing to exploit the new market opening in the EC. This is one reason why trade unions and other social groups are concerned lest the single market become a licence for capital to exploit differences in living standards and social rights to the detriment of workers and society at large.

The normal forces of the market-place, including the increased collective bargaining strengths of workers in the poorer EC economies may be expected, over time, to reduce the gap in living standards with the northern Member States. However this assumes not only that the poorer countries will be among the major beneficiaries of internal market decontrol and deregulation and that social wages will consequently increase but also that the 1990s will be years of relative economic expansion and not see a return to recession or 'stagflation'.

But action on the social wage is also a matter of public provision. It is bound to raise in a still sharper form the whole question of the redistribution of wealth between the richer and poorer parts of the Community. It would not be surprising to see pressure mount over the next decade for the EC to act to bring up social benefit and welfare rights standards (as well as provisions to protect the physical and social environment) closer to the best prevailing standards elsewhere in the Community. The greater the *de facto* economic integration of the EC the less tolerance there will be of major discrepencies in prevailing levels of social security provision.

---

6   Some interesting proposals on popular planning — including greater public consultation and involvement have already been aired. The European trade union movement has also begun discussions of international workers' plans for socially useful production lines initiated by workers in some large multinational companies in Britain and Germany. See *The Lucas Aerospace workers plan,* London, 1978.

At present the European Community decision-making institutions dispose of relatively marginal resources and powers in trying to make any significant impact on the wealth and development gap in the Community. But just as gross discrepencies between regions in one Member State are now a lively focus for political pressure and campaigning, the same should be expected between regions and countries within the EC in the last decade of this century. The conclusion seems inescapable. There will have to be a far larger European Community budget — in order to affect any significant redistribution of wealth — in the years after 1992.

Whatever the speed and direction of common social legislation in the European Community, there is surely no doubt that the achievement of the internal market in 1992 will give a far sharper profile to those issues which can loosely be summed up in the expression 'citizens' Europe'. Of course the 1992 legislation itself makes some provision in this area, notably for the right of free movement of people and the right to residential and professional establishment throughout the Community.

It will take longer than 1992 for all of this to become reality. This is all the more true given the opposition of some Member States to the wholesale dismantling of frontier controls. They are already pressing the case for national governments to have stronger controls in this area in order to be more effective in the fight against drugs, smuggling, terrorism and other crime.

Many experts already dispute the case that tighter frontier controls are the only or the most effective means of controlling crime or terrorism. Modern police methods of surveillance of cross-border crime are more sophisticated than they were 20 years ago and do not justify the maintenance of the whole paraphernalia of frontier checks and controls.

Indeed there appears to be more than a pinch of xenophobia in the way some politicians speak of the ending of frontier controls on the movement of people leading to mass, illegal immigration from Third World countries or risking the undermining of national rabies control.[7] It is unlikely, however, that most people in the European Community of the 1990s will be content with accepting that goods and money can move freely across borders while they, themselves, remain subject to tiresome and time-consuming frontier checks and controls. But the danger that the removal of internal border controls will be countered by tougher 'Fortress Europe' type controls over movement into the EC from outside countries cannot be ignored. It may be a different matter when the controls affect non-EC nationals. Civil libertarians are already concerned that the post-1992 EC frontier controls will discriminate against Third World migrants and those seeking political asylum.

The right for the people to move, live and work where they will within the Community may take time to fully achieve and it turns to an extent on the speed with which genuine mutual recognition of professional and other qualifications can be agreed. But on present trends it should be well on the way to being a reality even by the end of 1992.

Beyond 1992 the presence of even larger numbers of EC citizens living in Community countries other than where they were born is going to require major changes in national electoral law.

---

7   In October 1988 the European Commission unveiled new proposals for a campaign to eradicate rabies throughout the European Community and thus obviate the need for the kind of national frontier veterinary controls maintained by the UK and Irish Governments.

Already the Commission has proposed that all EC citizens, after a period of residential qualification and with some transitional phasing-in arrangements should be eligible to vote in local elections. Denmark, Belgium and the Netherlands have already made a start in giving non-nationals the right to vote in elections to the European Parliament.

It seems logical that, further down the line, the peoples of the Community should be free to vote in national elections either in the country of their origin or in their adopted country. But of course to the extent that the European Parliament acquires substantially increased powers in the years ahead, the European elections may come to seem at least equally as important as national general elections.

The already evident growth in the authority of the European Court of Justice seems certain to grow in the single European market. Indeed it may have to be substantially expanded in order to deal with the volume of litigation which is likely to be generated as a result of the Single European Act and the internal market because of the increasing flow of Community legislation.

If it is the case, as I have suggested earlier, that the Community will expand to embrace new Member States from Western — and possibly Eastern — Europe in the 1990s, a question mark must be placed over the viability of the Council of Europe in Strasbourg. There may well be a case for the Council of Europe itself, at least its ministerial manifestation, gradually withering away as more and more of its members accede to the Community. On the other hand, the role of the Court of Human Rights is likely to become more and not less important and maybe should, ultimately, be 'communitarized' and linked with the Court of Justice. The growing involvement of East European countries in the Council of Europe may also give it an enhanced function as a genuine pan-European forum.

It goes without saying that education and the media will play a critical role in the evolution of European society between now and the end of the century. For the time being education will remain overwhelmingly a responsibility of national governments but the success of the Community's work on student exchanges, particularly in higher education, and the growing interest in cooperation between educational authorities is here to stay. How long before our schools and colleges want to develop some common approach and syllabus such as European history or cultural studies?

We are already on the verge of a global communications revolution, particularly thanks to cable and satellite broadcasting and well before 1992 most television viewers in the Community are likely to have a vastly increased range of viewing choices. What remains to be seen is whether the technological marvels on modern communications will be matched by the right mixture of freedom and regulation to ensure that standards are improved and that unrestrained commercial competition does not reduce European television to a diet of pap in which current affairs, culture and quality programmes suffer.

The right of professional establishment and the mutual recognition of qualifications have now been agreed. But the emergence of a consumers' Europe is likely to be a speedier affair than the creation of a genuine citizens' Europe. Even that ignores the danger of the creation of a two-class Community — for instance in the field of the rights of movement and establishment — with migrant workers from outside the EC being relegated to an inferior class with fewer rights.

In the longer run however, comprehensive rights of movement, residence and work will almost certainly be achieved. Nor will any incipient two-class Community pass without challenge.

The next decade or two may also see closer coordination between different national educational systems. Indeed a start has been made in this direction with the Community's adoption of the Erasmus programme to encourage student exchanges.[8] More and more academics accept the need — in certain scientific and technological disciplines, but less certainly in the case of history — for a common European syllabus.

One major area of policy which is likely to undergo dramatic changeover in the next decade is foreign affairs and defence. Under the SEA, the European Community has already enhanced political cooperation to the point where Member States to all intents and purposes ensure that they are marching in step on all key foreign policy questions.

The Council of Ministers has also expanded its involvement in at least the political aspects of security policy — including discussions on arms- control strategy and future relations with the Soviet Union and its allies. The Community does not yet have a role in the strictly defence aspects of security policy, which for all Member States — other than neutral Ireland — is reserved for in NATO and the WEU.

There are signs that this might change. Even before the election of President Bush in the United States there has been increasing debate both in NATO and the WEU about a greater European self-sufficiency in defence and about the need to create a much stronger 'European-pillar' within the Atlantic Alliance.

One reason for this is the clear evidence that the US can no longer afford to carry the scale of financial burden involved in its present commitment to the defence of Western Europe. As we have noted, differences of perception of interest and judgment over key security and East/West issues have grown up in the past decade and these have been complicated and to some extent soured by commercial and economic frictions in the Atlantic relationship.

At the same time, the dramatic relaxation in tension between East and West since the advent of Mr Gorbachev in the Soviet Union has opened up potentially dramatic possibilities for *détente* and chemical, conventional and nuclear arms reduction agreements. There is a growing belief among European security strategists that the combination of these factors is likely to lead to an accelerating rundown in the US military presence in Western Europe over the next decade.

It remains to be seen whether this new transatlantic relationship is the result of mutual agreement or as a result of either an economic or political crisis within the Atlantic Alliance. Either way it raises some fascinating questions for Europeans to consider in the remaining years of this century.

For example, should the whole concept of a Soviet threat be reconsidered? Should Europeans resist or welcome the prospect of an accelerating denuclearization of their defences? Are Euro-

---

8   However an attempt to apply the principles of the Erasmus programme to language teaching and pupil exchange for school students was bitterly opposed by the UK Government and certain of the regional *Länder* administrations in the Federal Republic when it was proposed by the Commission in May 1989.

pean taxpayers willing, even in an era of *détente* and arms reductions, to finance the growing burden of defence spending at a time of so many competing claims for public resources?

Then there is the question of whether leadership of NATO which can become more genuinely double-headed as between Americans and Europeans. Some already believe the Community should gradually subsume the defence responsibilities which currently attach, as far as European NATO members are concerned, to the WEU.

On the face of it this is unlikely, at least, in the short run, partly because of the problem Ireland would face in agreeing to a European defence policy before the achievement of a full political union. But with other neutrals such as Austria suing for EC membership the character of the European Community's security philosophy is likely to be the subject of a major review.

On the other hand, the evolution of East/West relationship, the prospect of further and continuing arms reductions and the growing *de facto* independence of Eastern European States from the Soviet Union could totally change the nature of that security debate. If the Cold War is truly dying then Europe is going to have to undertake a fundamental redefinition of what it meant by European security in a multi-polar world. In future the goal of European reunification — from the Atlantic to the Urals — may not seem so utopian as in the past 50 years.

Of course there may be another scenario in which the failure of reform in the Soviet Union and Eastern Europe is followed by a recrudescence of Cold War tensions and new efforts by the superpowers to outbid each other in the nuclear arms race. But even in this depressing perspective it seems probable that Europeans will want to reconsider just what their own goals are and whether they can automatically be assumed to be identical with those of the United States.

It may be argued that we have strayed a long way from the immediate issues raised by the planned completion of the single European market and the abolition of internal frontiers. But in reality this market is both part of a wider agenda and a stimulant for developments which go well beyond the issues of a larger commercial market.

There is one major problem however with the kind of perspective for European development discussed above. Is it really going to be possible for the European Community to begin to tackle some of these medium and longer-term issues with its present decision-making structures?

What in essence is implied by gradual economic and monetary union, by an increasing European dimension for social, citizens' rights, foreign and security policy — to say nothing of full-scale political union — is the creation of a European State. The incipient trends towards the emergence of such a State have already been alluded to by leaders such as Mrs Thatcher in the current debates about 1992.

It is possible to take the position that nothing like this will ever happen, that a sense of cultural and political national identity will indefinitely prevent anything resembling political union. This book has argued that this is not the underlying trend of developments even though no one can predict the precise shape or timetable of an eventual European Union.

The Council of Ministers has been the institution whose power and authority has been most expanded as a result of the Single European Act. By comparison the enhanced management prerogatives of the Commission and the additional influence over legislation accorded to Members of the European Parliament are slight indeed.

Even before the completion of the 1992 single market it seems certain that European Parliamentarians are going to redouble their campaign to be given greater political power, not only over the Commission but more particularly over the Council of Ministers. Indeed in the campaign running up to the direct elections to the European Parliament — which took place in June 1989 — more calls were heard for MEPs to be given a bigger voice in shaping Community decisions.

It is hardly surprising that this is a burning issue for MEPs, if not, as yet, for the voting public. After all the present powers of Members of the European Parliament are a caricature of what would be normal in a democratic legislature. MEPs cannot even decide for themselves something as basic as where they will meet and where the Parliament will be headquartered.

The present grotesquely inefficient arrangement under which the European Parliament headquarters are in Luxembourg, the plenary sessions are held in Strasbourg and the key committees meet in Brussels are the outcome of a deal struck by national governments. They insist that any change must be agreed by unanimous decision of the 12 Governments, even though the European Court has opened a chink of light by ruling that for exceptional meetings the MEPs may decide to meet other than in Strasbourg.

The great majority do not want to be closeted in however pleasant an environment in Alsace, hundreds of kilometres from the principal decision-making institutions and the day-to-day executive of EC affairs which are in Brussels. Sooner or later the MEPs will defy the inter-governmental deal and, *de facto,* decamp to Brussels.

Observers tend to be equally surprised that the European Parliament is allowed no role in the selection and appointment of Members of the European Commission, which is also the sole prerogative of national governments. The MEPs can sack the Commission in its entirety — a largely theoretical and unusable power — but may not dismiss an individual Commissioner, however incompetent. It may be that if and when the Member States agree to revise the Rome Treaty to implement economic and monetary union MEPs will seize the opportunity to press for a greater role in determining regulation with the Council.

It is true that the European Parliament has lacked prestige and that it still lacks political legitimacy — partly because of the low and unenthusiastic turn-out of voters in European elections in at least some Member States. To the extent that this is a problem, it reflects lack of power, and hence lack of relevance to the lives of voters and citizens, of European Parliamentarians in past years.

Media coverage of European Parliament affairs tends to concentrate — notably in the popular mass circulation papers — on the more trivial and bizarre aspects of the lives of an admittedly highly paid, underworked and privileged coterie of Euro-Parliamentarians. But exotic irrelevance such as the odd expenses scandal, or the cost of needless and unproductive foreign trips by MEPs, are themselves a reflection of the vacuum created by the lack of political power and hence accountability to the electorate.

In theory it would be possible to try and turn the clock back and restore to national Parliaments the rights of amendment and rejection of EC legislation which were signed away when the Member States signed the Treaty of Accession on joining the Community. But this would not only be a process of nightmarish proportions both legally and politically but also would leave unresolved the question about how the views of each national Parliament should be reconciled so that a collective parliamentary view on EC policy proposals and directives could be achieved.

It is difficult, therefore, to see any radical progress towards common and improving standards of social and civil rights — even in a European Community single market — given the present grossly uneven development in the powers of the executive compared with the powers of parliamentary control in the European Community.

The position at present can hardly be tolerated for much longer. Real political power in the European Community is increasingly being exercised by the Council of Ministers, and only in a far more modest and subsidiary sense by the European Commission. In a sense the Council of Ministers is the real legislative body in the EC, in that it, and not the directly elected European Parliament, has the last word in passing laws which bind 320 million people.

Moreover, the Council takes its legislating decisions in private, behind closed doors and is not subject to direct scrutiny by the media or the general public. The theory is that since the Council is made up of the ministerial representatives of sovereign national governments, who are themselves answerable to democratic national Parliaments, that this is where the democratic scrutiny of Community affairs should take place.

It is true that most national Parliaments do attempt at least to scrutinize some EC legislation, although the volume of material now generated by the EC decision-making process is far beyond the capacity of a special committee of national Parliaments to digest and comment on. But even where this is possible, no national Parliament can alter or negate any decision of the Council once it is taken — that power was lost when each individual EC Member State signed the Treaty of Accession to the European Community.

This is one reason why the President of the Commission, Jacques Delors, was correct to warn that as the Community moves to 1992, belated realization of the powers now lost to national Parliaments might lead to a national backlash in some Member States against the whole concept of the European internal market.[9] But some national Parliaments do not yet understand that the power has been lost not to the European Parliament nor really to the Commission but directly to the Council of Ministers. Indeed the most effective way for national Parliamentarians to influence Community affairs in future will be in close cooperation with Members of the European Parliament.

Despite the mandate received from the electors in successive European elections and the enormous costs of operating a European Parliament, that body has not been given sufficient powers

---

9   He was speaking to the European Parliament in June 1988. In the months which followed an increasing number of MEPs, across the political spectrum, demanded a variety of measures to strengthen the role of the European Parliament and thus at least diminish a blatant and indefensible democratic deficit at the heart of Community affairs.

to enable proper surveillance and control of EC affairs. Indeed it is not allowed direct control, over the decisions of the Council — except over a narrow area dealing with the annual budget and the amendment of legislation — and it has no power either to appoint or remove the Council.

The reality is that the European Parliament for all its administrative and political faults, which are massive — above all its present nomadic existence between three different Community centres — Brussels, Luxembourg and Strasbourg — is a potentially far more effective democratic instrument to achieve these ends. European and national Parliamentarians actually share a common political interest in making the Council democratically accountable.

A new European Parliament with a new popular mandate from the Community's electorate will not for long be satisfied with its present very limited right to amend Community laws. The immediate goal is likely to be the achievement of a greater co-legislation right with the Council, of the kind pre-figured at present in a very narrow sense in the way the annual EC budget is drawn up.

There are several different ways in which a genuinely co-legislative system might work. In all variants however, MEPs would have to be given the final say in whether and in what form EC legislation is adopted.

If and when the Community does move to full and comprehensive political union there is a case for making the European Parliament the primary law-passing body — possibly, as at present on the initiative and proposal of the Commission. This would, of course, mean that the Commission would have to be elected by the Parliament and not, as at present nominated by national governments with no real consultation with European Parliamentarians.

One model for the longer-term future would be a bicameral European legislature within the elected or nominated representatives of the national States — and also the distinctive regions and minority communities within the EC — forming a sort of second chamber or upper house. The model here would be the Federal German Parliament with the directly elected Bundestag and the Bundesrat made up of representatives of the *Länder* — or regional governments.

In the short term MEPs should be accorded the right to select future Members of the Commission and should have the right to remove individual Commissioners as well as the entire executive. The Parliament should also have far greater rights of amendment and rejection of policies adopted by the Council — including all matters relating to political cooperation, where the rights of MEPs are almost totally non-existent.

More radical changes will probably have to wait on the development of popular demand from the mass of voters. But if the MEPs use the slight increase in their powers accorded by the SEA cleverly over the next four years, this should do much to give their deliberations far greater relevance to the general public and hence give the European Parliament greater political legitimacy.

The process is, however, inseparable from a sense of political conflict between the different parties and social movements in the Community. For it is this debate and conflict which imparts a sense of relevance and heightens public awareness of issues which are, at present, confined to a relative élite of Euro-specialists and enthusiasts in different walks of life.

It would be wrong to think that the debate about democracy and social change will necessarily have a narrow or exclusively Parliamentary focus. Europe 2000 may well be a society where the right of participation in decision-making is far more broadly diffused throughout industry and society. Interestingly this is the thrust of the demands being raised by advocates of radical restructuring in some East European countries as well.

Of course the question of democracy in the Europe of post-1992 and into the third millennium goes beyond purely parliamentary institutions. Europe has a long and rich history of struggle for social, economic and political emancipation and this is bound to have a reflection in the future in a wider economic and social democracy.

A genuinely united and democratic Europe could exercise a greater influence on world affairs and the emergence of the global community which is both necessary because of the crisis facing humanity and increasingly within our grasp. The future has no predetermined shape but is there to be shaped by the conscious actions of women and men.

For the first time in generations the peoples of Europe — all of Europe — are feeling their way to play their part in the creation of a better future. That, in the final analysis, is the true relevance of the debate which 1992 has made possible.

Works published in the

Document   series

Common standards for enterprises

Florence NICOLAS
with the cooperation of Jacques REPUSSARD

CB-PP-88-A01-EN-C

The single financial market

Dominique SERVAIS

CB-PP-88-C03-EN-C

A guide to working in a Europe without frontiers

Jean-Claude SÉCHÉ

CB-PP-88-004-EN-C

Freedom of movement in the Community
Entry and residence

Jean-Claude SÉCHÉ

CB-PP-88-B04-EN-C

Individual choice and higher growth
The task of European consumer policy

Eamonn LAWLOR

CB-PP-88-007-EN-C

1992 :
The European social dimension

Patrick VENTURINI

CB-PP-88-B05-EN-C

Works published in the

european perspectives
series

Telecommunications in Europe

Herbert UNGERER
with the collaboration of Nicholas P. COSTELLO

CB-PP-88-009-EN-C

The European Monetary System
Origins, operation and outlooks

Jacques van YPERSELE
with the collaboration of Jean-Claude KOEUNE

CB-PP-88-D03-EN-C

The European Communities
in the international order

Jean GROUX and Philippe MANIN

CB-40-84-206-EN-C

Money, economic policy and Europe

Tommaso PADOA-SCHIOPPA

CB-40-84-286-EN-C

The rights of working women in the European Community

Eve C. LANDAU

CB-43-85-741-EN-C

Lawyers in the European Community

CB-48-87-290-EN-C

Transport and European integration

Carlo degli ABBATI

CB-45-86-806-EN-C

Thirty years of Community law

Various authors

CB-32-81-681-EN-C

The Community legal order

Jean-Victor LOUIS

Second edition being prepared
CB-PP-88-016-EN-C

Also available:

European Economy — No 35

The economics of 1992

CB-AR-88-035-EN-C

European Economy — No 36

Creation of a European financial area

Liberalization of capital movements
and financial integration in the Community

CB-AR-88-036-EN-C

Social Europe — Special edition

The social dimension
of the internal market

CB-PP-88-005-EN-C

Energy in Europe — Special issue

The internal energy market

CB-PP-88-010-EN-C

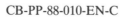

Research on the 'cost of non-Europe'

Basic findings
Volume **1**
Basic studies: executive summaries

CB-PP-88-B14-EN-C

Volume **2**
Studies on the economics of integration

CB-PP-88-C14-EN-C

Volume **3**
**The completion of the internal market:
a survey of European industry's perception
of the likely effects**

CB-PP-88-D14-EN-C

Basic studies: full reports
Volume 4
The 'cost of non-Europe'
— Border-related controls and administrative formalities: an illustration in the road haulage sector

CB-PP-88-E14-EN-C

Volume 5
The 'cost of non-Europe' in public sector procurement

CB-P1-88-F14-EN-C (Part A)
CB-P2-88-F14-EN-C (Part B)

Volume 6
— Technical barriers in the EC: an illustration by six industries
— The 'cost of non-Europe': some case studies on technical barriers

CB-PP-88-G14-EN-C

Volume 7
The 'cost of non-Europe':
Obstacles to transborder business activity

CB-PP-88-H14-EN-C

Volume 8
The 'cost of non-Europe' for business services

CB-PP-88-I14-EN-C

Volume **9**

The 'cost of non-Europe' in financial services

CB-PP-88-J14-EN-C

Volume **10**

The benefits of completing the internal market for telecommunications services and equipment in the Community

CB-PP-88-K14-EN-C

Volume **11**

The EC 1992 automobile sector

CB-PP-88-L14-EN-C

Volume **12**

The 'cost of non-Europe' in the foodstuffs industry

CB-P1-88-M14-EN-C (Part A)
CB-P2-88-M14-EN-C (Part B)

Volume **13**

Le 'coût de la non-Europe' des produits de construction

CB-PP-88-N14-FR-C

Volume 14
The 'cost of non-Europe'
in the textile/clothing industry

CB-PP-88-014-EN-C

Volume 15
The 'cost of non-Europe'
in pharmaceutical industry

CB-PP-88-P14-EN-C

Volume 16
The internal markets of North America
Fragmentation and integration in the USA and Canada

CB-PP-88-Q14-EN-C

European Communities — Commission

1992 and beyond

by John Palmer

Luxembourg: Office for Official Publications of the European Communities

1989 — 95 pp. — 17.6 × 25.0 cm

Document series

ES, DA, DE, GR, EN, FR, IT, NL, PT

ISBN 92-826-0088-2

Catalogue number: CB-56-89-861-EN-C

Price (excluding VAT) in Luxembourg: ECU 8